NEW YORK

BONECHI & CITY MERCHANDISE

Worlds Greatest Souvenirs

CITY MERCHANDISE INC.
228 40th Street
Brooklyn, N.Y. 11232
Tel. 718 - 832 - 2931
Fax 718 - 832 - 2939
E-mail: citymerchandise@aol.com
Http: www. citymerchandise.com

© Copyright by Casa Editrice Bonechi - Florence - Italy
Publication created by Casa Editrice Bonechi. Publication manager: Monica Bonechi
Photographic research by the Editorial Staff of the Casa Editrice Bonechi
Graphic design and layout: Manuela Ranfagni. Cover: Manuela Ranfagni and Rosanna Malagrinò. Editing: Anna Baldini
Drawings on pages 32, 38, 39, 40 by Stefano Benini. Maps on pages 34 and 50 by Daniela Mariani.
Texts by Robert Fitzgerald, Giovanna Magi, Maria Elena Velardi, and the Editorial Staff of Casa Editrice Bonechi.
Translations by Paula Boomsliter and Julia Weiss.

PHOTO CREDITS
Photographs from the Casa Editrice Bonechi Archives. By Marco Bonechi: pages 20/21, 51 bottom, 52, 60/61, 70, 73, 86 bottom, 91.
By Paolo Giambone: 47, 63 bottom, 64, 66 top, 68 bottom right, 70, 73, 79.
By Andrea Pistolesi: pages 3, 5 bottom, 8/9, 24, 27, 28 bottom right, 32, 34, 35, 36/37, 40, 41, 44, 45, 48 right, 49, 51 top, 53, 54, 55, 56, 57, 62, 63 top, 66 bottom, 67, 78, 80, 81, 82, 83, 84, 85, 87, 88/89, 90, 92, 93, 94, 95.

Alan Schein/NYC: pages 26, 28 top and bottom left, 29, 42 top, 43 top right and bottom left, 46.
American Museum of Natural History: pages 68 bottom left and 69 bottom left (© Scott Frances) / page 69 top (© J. Beckett/AMNH) / page 69 bottom right (© J. Beckett/D. Finnin).
© Archimation: page 7 bottom right. Associated Press, AP: pages 10(Ph. Jim Wells, Staff), 11, 12, 13 top(Ph. Marty Lederhandler, Staff), 13 bottom, 15 left(Ph. Stringer), 15 right(Ph. Alan Welner, Stringer), 16 (Ph. Richard Drew, Staff). Battman Studios: pages 22/23, 30/31, 43 right center.
© Bedford/Downing (Igor Maloratsky Ph.): pages 42 center (#800) and right (#806), 48 left (#901). ©Collection of The New-York Historical Society: pages 33 bottom, 39 center. Eric Van Den Brulle: page 74 top.
Foto Scala, Firenze: pages 74,75,76. Frank De Sisto/ Intrepid Sea-Air-Space Museum: page 65. Newsday Photo/Paul Bereswill: page 58 bottom.
Courtesy of NY Mets: page 58 center. Courtesy of NY Yankees: page 58 top. Realy Easy Star, Turin: pages 71, 72 left center and bottom, 72 right center (Maurizio Stabio),77 top. Romana Javitz Collection. Miriam and Ira D. Wallach Division of Art, Prints & Photographs. The New York Public Library: pages 33 top and center. Courtesy of Settore Cultura del Comune di Prato: page 4 top left (painting by Orazio Fidani).
State Historical Society of Wisconsin by Courtesy of the Ellis Island Immigration Museum: page 5 top and center.
© Studio Daniel Libeskind: page 7 bottom center. © Torsten Seidel: page 7 bottom left.

ACKNOWLEDGMENTS
The photograph on page 17 was taken by Maria Elena Velardi of our New York office, which is located near the site of the World Trade Center. Our heartfelt thanks to all the television cameramen, photographers, and Internet sites (CNN, BBC, Time Magazine, The New York Times, Virgilio, Altavista) whence come the images on pages 18, 19.

For certain images it was not possible to trace the original source. The Publisher apologizes for these omissions and makes himself available for all additions, when informed from the rightful owners.

ISBN 88-476-1189-X

NEW YORK
The Birth of a Metropolis

When describing New York, it is nearly impossible not to run out of superlatives at some point, and although Manhattan, with its bare 22 square miles (57 square km) of territory, is only the third largest of the city's boroughs, it truly offers something for everyone.

New York is, first of all, a city on the water, made up of five boroughs. Manhattan and Staten Island are completely circumscribed by water. Brooklyn and Queens occupy the western tip of the ocean-reaching Long Island; the Bronx is on a peninsula, surrounded by water on three sides. The city's bay and its rivers not only form the largest and most extraordinary natural port in the world, but have also, always, contributed to stimulating the city's unstoppable growth. Each year, the Big Apple welcomes about 25 million tourists, few of whom fail to feel the sheer energy that pulsates along its streets and avenues.

Uptown, down Broadway and across Times Square, all the way south to the Village, SoHo, and the port, its dynamism is a palpable force. The streets, the subways, the department stores, the buildings—and among them the skyscrapers—the restaurants and stores of all kinds and nationalities, the theaters: everything in this city, cosmopolitan par excellence, contributes to composing a totally unique and dazzling scenario that leaves any visitor with a sense of incredulity.

The population of this "world capital" has always been made up of people from every conceivable country and of communities of different races and religions. At the end of the 19th century, Ellis Island, off the extreme southern tip of Manhattan, was receiving and "processing" 5,000 immigrants per day—all destined to become new American citizens. The cultural multiplicity and disregard of convention that characterize New York make it a place like no other in the world. And the tag "New Yorker" is a special designation even within the United States. The uniqueness of this city is apparent at first glance. The sense of power is overwhelming, and is due mainly to the skyscrapers that impertinently challenge the clouds. Since 1903, seven of these giants have, one after the other, boasted of being the world's tallest. Penetrating the shadows of the canyons they define can be a disconcerting experience, because at street level there reigns a chaos of honking yellow cabs, frenetic pedestrians, and

GIOVANNI DA VERRAZZANO
(Verrazzano 1485 – Brazil 1528)

The great navigator was born in 1485 in Verrazzano, 20 kilometers from Florence, descendent of an old Tuscan family. Adventurous of spirit, from his youth he was impatient to set out to explore new worlds. At the beginning of the XVI century, due to political disputes between his family and the Medici government, he moved to France and settled at Dieppe, the port on the English Channel. There he met skilled sailors and ship owners and learned from them. In 1523 he set out, in the service of the king of France, Francis I, leading an expedition sailing "west to explore the Orient" and its promising markets. He crossed the Atlantic Ocean on board the "Dauphine" and reached Florida. Then he sailed north along the coast searching for the passage to the Pacific Ocean and discovered the estuary of what is now called the Hudson River.
On **17 April 1524** he sailed into New York harbor and landed on the island of Manhattan, a wild area, probably inhabited by Algonquin Indians. The navigator was in great demand by the enemies of France, but he remained loyal to the King and undertook many other expeditions. He died in Brazil, probably killed by the natives, in 1528.
New York named the **Verrazzano Narrows–Bridge** after the great navigator. The world's longest suspension bridge (opened in 1964) crosses the entrance to New York Harbor known as the Narrows.

flashing lights. New York is known world over for the unmistakable, soaring profiles that define its skyline. The skyscrapers are not only major tourist attractions in the Big Apple—they are also this city's most important contribution to the history of architecture. Just a few square miles enclose a fascinating architectural itinerary from the late 19th century through our times, with a variety of styles going from the neo-Gothic of the Woolworth Building to the Deconstructivist architecture of the recent Condé Nast Building. Less evident—but of fundamental importance—are the engineering innovations introduced by the designers and builders: from the invention of the elevator to the erection of the first metal load-bearing structures. The lure of the skyscraper lies in its audacious combination of all these elements in a highly visible tribute to 20th century human ingenuity. The Empire State Building, the New Yorkers' best-loved skyscraper, relinquished its title as the city's tallest decades ago, but together with the Statue of Liberty remains the globally-recognized symbol of this great cosmopolitan metropolis.

The Origins of Today's "Big Apple"

Trade, and the search for new markets and products, brought the Europeans to the New World and to New York. The city founders were merchants; since its beginnings, the city has been an important commercial node on the "new" continent.
In 1524, the Italian explorer Giovanni da Verrazano landed on the coast of what is today New York City during his search for a Northwest Passage to the Orient. Only later, in 1609, did Henry Hudson sail the river which now takes his name, and so officially launch colonization.
The first colonists—Belgians, and later the Dutch—began to arrive in 1624. A year later, the Dutch West India Company erected the first "official" building in New Amsterdam. Then, in 1626, Peter Minuit, the city's first Director-General, "purchased" the territory of Manhattan Island from the Canarsee tribe for—as legend has it—tools and clothes worth about 24 dollars.
In 1702, Manhattan became British territory and Queen Anne appointed her

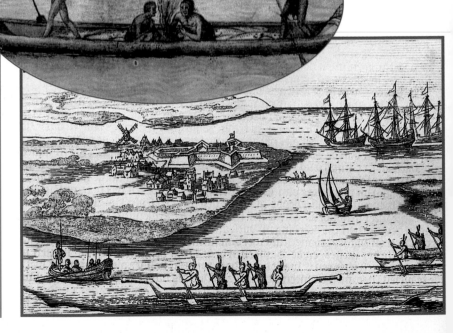

*Opposite page: bottom: **Manhattan**, in one of the oldest views of New York, shortly after the founding of the Dutch settlement (1626) symbolized by the windmill. Center: a reconstruction of what Indian life must have been like on the island of Manhattan when Peter Minuit purchased it from the local tribe.*

*Historic photos of **Ellis Island** where the nation's main immigration center was established at the end of the XIX century: above the island and one of the rooms where immigrants were processed; left: a group of immigrants.*

*Below: bird's eye view of Ellis Island and the **Museum of Immigration** that conserves documents on the great phenomenon that brought millions of people from all over the world to the United States.*

cousin Lord Cornbury as the first Governor of New York. In 1776, during the American Revolution, the British burned Manhattan, but despite this New York was the capital of the new nation from 1785 through 1790. On 23 April 1789, George Washington was sworn in as the US's first President on the terrace of Federal Hall. Since then, New York has remained a "capital" in many respects, and in 1835 survived the Great Fire that destroyed a goodly portion of Lower Manhattan, rising again from the ashes more splendid than ever.
A golden age began for the city at the end of the Revolutionary War. In just a few years New York became the largest city in the United States and by 1830 the largest on the continent, thanks above all to its port, which landed not only goods but also millions of immigrants in search of fortune. Development of the city in the 19th

century was in fact characterized by such a massive influx of European immigrants that in the second half of the century the majority of the city's

residents were people who had been born abroad. The new arrivals congregated mainly in the southern part of Manhattan island, creating

*A period photo of the **Brooklyn Bridge** that was opened on 24 May 1883 and a panorama of New York in the 'Forties with the towering spires of the **Empire State Building**, the tallest (1931) and the **Chrysler Building** (1930) – third from the left.*

*Left: a historic shot of **Fifth Avenue**.*

ethnic quarters that maintained their peculiar identities for more than a century, like the Lower East Side of the European Jews, Little Italy, and Chinatown. In the meantime, New York was expanding northwards. In 1857, construction of Central Park (the first urban park designed in the United States) was assigned to the landscape architects Frederick Law Olmsted and Calvert Vaux. After two years' work by 20,000 workers, the park was inaugurated in the winter of 1859. It immediately became one of the city's major attractions, with more than 7 million visitors in its first year. In 1860 the combined populations of Manhattan and the adjacent Brooklyn topped the one million mark. During the 19th century, New York was transformed into the great cosmopolitan metropolis we know today thanks to booming commerce and the introduction of many new technologies that made it possible to manage a city of such proportions. Among these were gas and then electrical lighting, a public transport system, and what was, at the time, the largest and most efficient aqueduct in the world. The symbol par excellence of this phase in the city's history is without a doubt the Brooklyn Bridge (1883), which is still considered a masterpiece of modern engineering.

In 1898 a public referendum approved incorporation of Manhattan, Queens, Brooklyn, Staten Island, and the Bronx as a single municipality, bringing the city's population to almost 3.5 million inhabitants. In the early 20th century, the city experienced its second golden age thanks to the affirmation of Wall Street as the economic and financial center of the country. These were the years of legendary figures in US economic history like the financier John P. Morgan and the entrepreneurs John D. Rockefeller, Andrew Carnegie, and Frank W. Woolworth, who founded the first great American dynasties; these were the years of the Chrysler Building and the Empire State Building. This positive phase in the city's history came to a brusque end in the early 1930's with the onset of the Great Depression. The New Deal launched by President Franklin D. Roosevelt, a former governor of New York State, helped the city to emerge from the crisis; later, World War II created jobs in the city, and especially in and around Brooklyn's important shipyards.

Beginning in 1945, the face of the city began to change as it lost many of its industrial activities and services took the upper hand. In the 1950's and 60's a new boom in development gave New York its Rockefeller Center and Lincoln Center, while the idea of a World Trade Center began to take hold. Construction of the Twin Towers complex lasted from 1971 to 1976. The world economic crisis of the 1970's was felt in New York; in 1975 the city was on the verge of bankruptcy due to its enormous deficit. Thanks to a federal loan, the city recovered and by the early 1980's was already well on the road to prosperity. At the end of the 20th century, New York was the international symbol of the great cosmopolitan metropolis, but the World Trade Center had become the target for terrorist attacks by the Islamic integralist forces that opposed the economic system and the culture developed in the Western world.

The Twin Towers were attacked twice. In 1993 a bomb in a van in the parking garage of the complex caused six deaths, but the second attack, on September 11, 2001, caused the collapse of both towers and the loss of about 2,800 lives. This tragic event was a turning point not only in the history of the city but in that of the entire world.

GROUND ZERO: THE RECONSTRUCTION

Memory Foundations is the name of the project by Daniel Libeskind who, less than 18 months after the tragedy, won the competition to rebuild the site of the World Trade Center. The group of irregular polygon buildings will include a sunken space in the foundations of the WTC, a Museum and a Memorial Park where every year on 11 September the sun will shine without casting any shadows between 8:46 a.m. (the time of the first attack) and 10:28 a.m. (when the second tower collapsed). With the construction of the Antenna Tower New York will reclaim the title of hosting the world's tallest building: its spire with the vertical garden will reach a height of 1,776 feet (541.3 meters). This drawing shows the general plans for the reconstruction. It will most probably be modified during construction to meet the needs of the various political, commercial and social groups who – as in the case of the Twin Towers – are involved in this historic project. In any event, the **Memorial** dedicated to the victims of September 11th will be the heart of the new World Trade Center.

The World Trade Center and the Twin Towers

The History of a Symbol

Visible from afar and unique in the world in the elegance of their simple duplicity, for nearly thirty years from their dedication the Twin Towers were a portal, a cornice, a dual beacon over the fabulous city that is New York. From their observation decks, tourists enjoyed a magnificent view of the entire city and its port—and the Statue of Liberty. Despite never having earned favor with the experts, their unmistakable silhouette immediately became a worldwide symbol of the Big Apple.

The towers were also a popular stop on the tourist circuit: like the Empire State Building, they were never mere office buildings or skyscrapers striving upward toward a place in the record books; like the Empire State, the Towers-that-were expressed the spirit of an important era in New York's history.

But they also introduced technical innovations in construction science and engineering. The WTC design team was headed by the architect Minoru Yamasaki, who consulted with Emery Roth & Sons, a renowned architectural firm with extensive experience with buildings of this type in New York City. Actual construction took seven years, and by the time the Twin Towers were inaugurated in 1973 they were already a dominant feature of the skyline. Speaking to the broader historical context, the World Trade Center was conceived in the post-WWII period as a symbol of the prosperity and success achieved by the United States at the global level. And as a symbol of late 20th century American spirit, the Towers became the target of terrorist attacks, which culminated in their tragic destruction on September 11, 2001.

and the Twin Towers

*Construction of one of the **Twin Towers**, October 20, 1970. In the background at right is the **Empire State Building** with its antenna.*

*On the facing page, the **World Trade Center** towers seen from above during construction. The space reserved for the elevators is clearly visible at the center of the North Tower.*

From the Foundations to the Observation Decks: the Building of a Symbol of an Era

The idea of building a "world trade center" as an expression of the spirit of enterprise—or, according to your point of view, of American economic predomination after World War II—began to take hold in the 1950s. The promoters of the initiative saw the center as a place where the most prestigious public and private concerns in international commerce would be united under a single roof, as it were. The WTC would have celebrated the miracle of New York and its port, which in the 19th and 20th centuries had made a considerable fortune for the metropolis. Since the very beginning, the WTC complex had its brutal detractors and impassioned supporters. It is significant that the building and management of the World Trade Center complex was entrusted to a public body, the Port Authority of New York and New Jersey (PANYNJ) instead of one of the private construction firms that have always dominated the real estate panorama in the city—and above all the eternal competition for the tallest skyscraper. The project in fact encountered stiff opposition from important New York

entrepreneurs, who feared a collapse of real estate values in the city; they were joined on their bandwagon by politicians who would have preferred other investment destinations for the hundreds of millions of dollars earmarked for the WTC. And this explains why four years passed between official approval for construction, granted on March, 27 1962 by New York State Governor Nelson A. Rockefeller, and the actual start of work.

In 1966, the demolition of the old buildings on 16 acres of land bounded by Vesey Street, Liberty Street, Church Street, and West Street marked the start of construction. The massive technical problems inherent in the project were brilliantly resolved by the PANYNJ engineers and their collaborators. First of all, in order to lay safe foundations, the builders had to excavate to about 23 meters (70 feet) to reach bedrock. At the same time, they had to waterproof the construction site against seepage, since the land had originally been river-bottom and had been created by landfills—making use of materials from demolished buildings and even

abandoned ships—over the years. Another problem, how to dispose of the million cubic meters of excavated material, was resolved by reusing it as landfill: this time to extend the shoreline of the southwestern tip of Manhattan Island to create developable land, valued at 90 million dollars, which later became the site of the exclusive Battery Park City. Construction of buildings so tall in an area exposed to strong winds raised yet another set of problems. But the engineers had a solution: while traditional skyscrapers are built around internal load-bearing columns, the Twin Towers plans called for a load-carrying external "lattice" of high-resistance steel and tempered glass. There are two noteworthy advantages to this type of structure: first of all, it is resistant to lateral wind loads, and secondly, it leaves vast, completely unencumbered and well-lit areas of internal floor space that command high rents. The first section of the exterior walls of the North Tower were erected in August 1968, and from then onward construction progressed in phases, accurately synchronized with delivery of the construction materials. The last technical problem faced by the engineers and Yamasaki was represented by the elevators, to which fell the unenviable daily task of moving tens of thousands of workers and visitors up and down among the 110 floors of the towers. The innovative skylobby system, a combination of local and express elevator banks, not only resolved the traffic problem but considerably reduced the space required for installing the elevators, all to the benefit of incrementing rentable floor space. The first tenants occupied the offices on the lower floors of the North Tower in 1970, while work on the upper

The still-unfinished **Twin Towers** already soared above New York's other skyscrapers, June 13, 1970. The turreted **Woolworth Building** (1913) and the **Municipal Building** (1914), seemingly right in front of it, are clearly identifiable.

Bottom, an other image of the Twin Towers during construction. Both towers will be **110 stories** tall.

stories was still in progress. The North Tower was completed in December of 1970; the South Tower seven months later. The official opening was celebrated in 1973, when the interiors were finished. At that time, the World Trade Center was without a doubt the world's most advanced office complex, equipped with a broadband telecommunications system, air conditioning, and a state-of-the-art elevator system. As the years went by, the World Trade Center became a true city-within-a-city, boasting hotel accommodations (the Marriot at 3WTC), covered parking facilities, restaurants, shops, and even a day care center.

The Observation Decks

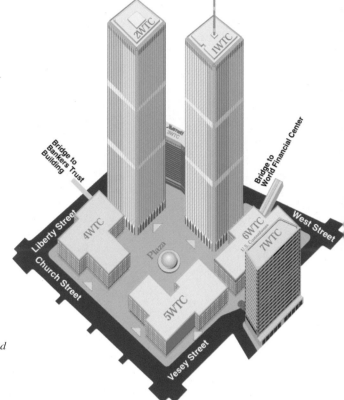

Given the enormous popularity of the Empire State Building as a belvedere on New York, the World Trade Center designers only naturally thought to include two glassed-in observation decks in their plans, one on the 107th floor of the South Tower, open to the general public, and another, destined to hold an exclusive luxury restaurant, in the North Tower. The decision immediately proved to be the right one, and the one-millionth observation deck visitor was feted less than a year after the deck opened. The Windows on the World restaurant, inaugurated in 1976 on the 107th floor of the North Tower, immediately became one of New York's most fashionable dining rooms. Both observatories, plus the roof deck of the South tower, were the locations for photo reportages, wedding celebrations, exclusive parties, and the like, and were soon high on the list of "musts" for tourists and New Yorkers alike.

*The buildings of the **World Trade Center** complex, today destroyed or severely damaged: **1WTC** or North Tower; **2WTC** or South Tower; **3WTC**, Marriott Hotel; **4WTC**, Commodities Exchange; **5WTC**, Northeast Plaza Building; **6WTC**, U.S. Customs House; **7WTC**, Tishman Center.*

Daredevils et al.

*D*uring their lifetimes, the Twin Towers were witness to many spectacular events. Since the very first, thanks to their vertiginous heights and the peculiar conformation of the complex, they were the venue for a number of daring feats. The first was perpetrated by the funambulist **Philippe Petit**, who on the morning of August 7, 1974 left thousands of spectators gaping as he walked a cable strung between the tops of the two towers. The next year it was base jumping: **Owen Quinn** jumped off the 110th floor of the North Tower, opening his parachute at a mere 250 meters (820 ft) from the ground. In 1977, the summit of the North Tower was finally conquered, after months of preparation and an actual climb of 3 1/2 hours. But the 27-year-old **George Willig**, nicknamed the "Human Fly," was not the only climber to venture up one of the towers. In 1976 an old acquaintance of New York's skyscrapers, the ill-starred **King Kong**, scaled the WTC in the finale of the remake of the movie with Jessica Lange. Only a few years after their inauguration, the Twin Towers were already world-level popular icons.

George Willig, the "human fly," is watched from the streets and skyscrapers of Lower Manhattan, May 26, 1977

*The funambulist **Philippe Petit**, August 7, 1974.*

February 26, 1993

Just as they aroused admiration as the symbol of US economic achievement, in the 1990's the Twin Towers became the preferred target of international anti- American terrorism. The first attack was on February 26, 1993, when a van packed with explosives detonated in the North Tower garage, blasting a crater three stories deep. The devastation, while considerable, was limited to the garage area and did not harm the supporting structures of the building, but the explosion inevitably caused panic in both towers.

The bomb was in fact so placed as to cause maximum damage and cut off the electricity to the entire complex. There were about 50,000 people in it at the time. It took almost twelve hours to evacuate all those trapped in the North Tower. The explosion caused the deaths of six and wounded about a thousand, among whom more than one hundred fire-fighters. Nonetheless tragic, the casualties would have been astounding had the terrorists succeeded in their original intent to topple one tower into the other and free a cloud of cyanide gas. Repairs were completed in a year's time. The attack's chief deviser, Ramzi Ahmed Yousef, was captured in 1995 and is currently serving a life sentence in the US. The same Al-Quaeda terrorist group, led by the fanatic Osama Bin-Laden, organized the second tragic attack that on September 11, 2001 caused the collapse of both towers and thousands of deaths. This attack is considered the most devastating terrorist attack ever launched anywhere in the world. The images of that tragic morning on which two airliners crashed into the towers are still etched in our memories and will not be easily forgotten.

A crater in an underground parking garage from the **World Trade Center** *explosion is shown in this file photo taken Saturday, February 27,* **1993**.

ist Attacks
September 11, 2001

At 8:46 a.m. on Tuesday, September 11, 2001, the unmistakable profile of downtown Manhattan changed forever.

The World Trade Center, icon of the economic power of the United States, symbol of American pride, a city rising vertically within another city, crumbled, pulverized in the span of "just" ninety minutes. The terrifying chronicle of the most serious terrorist attack in history began in the heart of New York City, where every day fifty thousand individuals worked nine to five in offices on the 110 floors of steel and glass that were the structure of the Twin Towers; where every day eighty thousand visitors were ferried up and down the height of the towers—at the fantastic speed of about 25 feet (8m)/second—by 208 elevators. Up there, at the top, was Windows On the World. The WTC brochure and the tourist guides proclaimed it the "world's highest restaurant," the only place to dine with your head—literally—in the clouds.

Over 1400 feet below (459 m) were all the suggestive lights of Manhattan; you could see much of the Hudson and the East River, and the Brooklyn Bridge. From up there, even the 843 acres of Central Park looked like somebody's back yard.

Up there you couldn't help—if only for a moment—but remember King Kong and his desperate, last

*The **North Tower**, in the heart of New York's Financial District, was hit at the 87th-floor level by the first Boeing 767, September 11, **2001**.*

embrace of the towers in the remake of the movie. Up there, inevitably, you found yourself humming a tune made famous by Liza Minnelli, because up there you really did feel you were "king of the hill, top of the heap."

Or you stopped in at the souvenir shop to take away a tiny bite of the Big Apple.

It might have been one of those plastic balls that scatter snow on a miniature Manhattan, complete with its Towers, its Empire State Building, and its Statue of Liberty all crowded together in an improbable cityscape.

Or it might have been a book, a calendar, a tee-shirt, a postcard sent to friends with a penned-in arrow pointing at the top floor to show that "we" had really been up there.

From "up there" it was great fun to look "down there" and remark on the apparent size of the cars, the people, the other buildings, which seemed so small that after a while you couldn't wait to get your feet back on the ground and resume your normal "human" proportions. There was just one way to photograph the Towers: to back up step by step from the World Trade Center with your camera aimed as high as it would go until they came into the viewfinder of your typical tourist camera.

The numbers that made the history and drew the portrait of the Twin Towers—their height, the number of windows, the millions of dollars spent, the tons of material, the miles of electrical cables—are worthy of entry in the Guinness Book of Records, without exception. Today they have been erased to make space for other, sinister numbers: the number of dead and wounded, the number of those who will recover, the number of people whose bodies and souls will carry the scars of that day for who knows how long.

The idea informing the work of Minoru Yamasaki, the Japanese architect who designed the towers, was that they become a concrete symbol of man's confidence in Man. In the light of the terrible events that changed Manhattan's skyline, we cannot help but ask ourselves what else collapsed at 10:07 and 10:28 on Tuesday, September 11, 2001, together with the Twin Towers of the World Trade Center. Maybe the towers will be rebuilt. Maybe there will remain a space, an open wound, a scar to remind us of something we ought never to forget.

But even though the two skyscrapers have been as if plucked out of the Manhattan skyline, they will always remain in our hearts. No act of barbarism, even the cruelest, can ever truly destroy the works of civilized man.

The media images of the terrorist attack in New York brought the most dramatic live news chronicle of our times into everyone's homes.

At 8:46, under the astonished gazes of the thousands of people who were setting about their everyday activities on a morning seemingly just like any other, an American Airlines passenger jet hijacked by a commando unit of terrorists, veered off course and flew straight into one of the towers of the World Trade Center in the heart of downtown Manhattan. Eighteen minutes later, while the cameras of the world's broadcasting companies were focusing on the nightmarish images of the smoke and flames pouring out of the north tower, another plane made a direct hit on the other tower.

The two airliners had been transformed into missiles, their unaware and guiltless passengers into human warheads directed against targets filled with likewise unaware and guiltless citizens.

The death throes of the two giant buildings lasted an hour and a half. During this time, inside the towers, there were played out human dramas and tragedies later documented by the voices of the survivors, the reports of the rescue workers, the images snapped by the photographers who despite their equal sense of horror immortalized the heartbreaking cries for help, the desperate gestures dictated by panic, the last moments in the lives of scores and scores of human beings. Many, to escape the hell of the

flames, threw themselves from the windows of the upper floors. Those ninety long minutes decided the fates of thousands of people who just because they happened to be there, on that day, at that time, trapped in what until September 11 had been an office building like any other.

The lucky ones who escaped the terrible impact of the planes or who were not isolated on the top floors began the long descent to safety down the stairs: ninety minutes, an eternity for those used to a short elevator ride between their offices and the street.

At 10:07 the world watched, impotent, as the south tower collapsed, and twenty minutes later as the second of the giants fell. They were simply gone, crumbled into an immense cloud of dust and smoke that spread across New York, almost as a merciful shroud.

The old and the new in a dramatic image of the September 11th terrorist attack: the Empire State Building against the background of the stricken Twin Towers.

The tragic sequence of the terrorist attack that changed the face of New York.

The Architectural Controversy

*T*he architectural community was never very enthusiastic about the Twin Towers, perhaps because the prevailing culture at PANYNJ was engineering-oriented and the project was entrusted, rather than to an architect's architect, to **Minoru Yamasaki**, who more than others was disposed to cooperate with the engineers and to follow PANYNJ directives as to volumes and use of space. Like other architects of the time, the American-born Yamasaki, of Japanese descent, was exploring alternatives to the International style that had dominated in world architecture for thirty years. He was a follower of **Neo-Formalism**, a style that remained a secondary current after the explosion of Post-Modernism in the 1970s. Among the tenets of Neo-Formalism were recovery of pleasing ornamental details and rebuttal of the "all-glass" facades typical of the International style. Other works by Minoru Yamasaki include the McGregor Memorial Conference Center in Detroit, the U.S. science pavilion for the 1962 Seattle World Exposition, and Los Angeles' Century Plaza Hotel. Yamasaki was awarded the commission to design the World Trade Center in 1962; after hundreds of sketches, he produced a final plan for two towers on an open plaza, surrounded by five additional buildings. In the initial plan, the towers were to rise to between 80 and 90 floors, but the PANYNJ was committed to building the world's tallest skyscrapers, and so it was: 110 floors in the final model. Structures of this size called for strict cooperation with engineering experts; one result was the introduction of important innovations, like the load-carrying exterior steel columns and lattice walls and narrow, full-floor height recessed windows that permitted maximum visibility from the inside without creating sensations of vertigo. As we mentioned above, many architects snubbed the complex, but its enormous popular success was surely a cause for boasting by its creators.

In the Past as in the Present:
an International Port

Half of the area on which the World Trade Center complex stood was originally under the port of Manhattan, and a number of interesting finds were brought to light during excavations for the foundations. Among these were the remains of the Dutch trading ship Tiger, sunk in 1613 after a fire on board, and of the Washington Market building, a fixture of 19th-century Lower Manhattan—and cannonballs, ancient anchors, and a plethora of bottles, shoes, pipes, and other ordinary objects lost or disposed of in the river. All of these finds bear witness to how since its earliest days the extreme downtown area has always been a busy hub of commerce—and only reinforced the idea that a center for international trade was the most fitting crown for "Manhattan's business tip."

The Kangaroo Cranes

One of the many technical problems faced by the WTC engineers—and certainly one of the most important—was how to get all the construction materials "up there." The NY-NJ Port Authority contacted an Australian concern specialized in powerful cranes—the so-called "kangaroos"— that once placed in the elevator shafts of a building can "go up" as the building does.

*A panorama of Manhattan with the **Brooklyn Bridge** in the foreground, after the collapse of the Twin Towers.*

Twin Towers Stats

Height North Tower (1WTC)	**417 meters (1368 ft)**
Height South Tower (2WTC)	**415 meters (1362 ft)**
Dimensions at Base	**63.4 x 63.4 meters (208 x 208 ft)**
Aboveground Floors	**110**
Underground Floors	**7**
Cost of Construction	**US$ 1.5 billion**
Steel Used in Construction (total WTC)	**185,000 tons**
Total Construction Workers	**7,500**
Deaths in Construction Accidents	**8**
Total Windows on Twin Towers	**43,600**
Elevators per Tower	**97 passenger + 6 freight**
Passenger Elevator Capacity	**55 persons**
Underground Parking	**for 2000 vehicles**
Transmitting Antenna Height (1WTC)	**104 meters (360 ft)**

Skyscrapers

The Giants of New York

FLATIRON
(Fuller Building)
1902 *(285 ft/87 meters)*
WOOLWORTH BUILDING
1913 *(782 ft/241 meters)*
CHRYSLER BUILDING
1930 *(1130 ft/319 meters)*
EMPIRE STATE BUILDING
1931 *(1247 ft/381 meters)*
GE BUILDING
(Rockefeller Center)
1940 *(850 ft/259 meters)*
METLIFE BUILDING
1963 *(801 ft/246 meters)*
TWIN TOWERS
1972-73
(1379 ft/417 –1362 ft/415 meters)
TRUMP TOWER
1983 *(657 ft/202.5)*

More than one hundred years have passed since the construction of the first skyscraper, but the New York panorama continues to change and change. The passions aroused by these towers that seem to touch the sky has not diminished. Different generations of architects have tested themselves against this type of building applying new architectural styles, creating daring structures, using new materials, and proposing original solutions. New York is a city that is built upwards. Walking along the streets amidst these still concrete giants can be an intimidating experience because seen from the sidewalk their bulk seems inhuman and sometimes it is even difficult to see the tops. However, it is sufficient to change perspective and go up to the observatories to enjoy a fascinating view that will let you appreciate the talent and commitment that made these structures possible. It is impossible to forget that behind each of these giants there are always people, and looking at their creations we can perceive the dreams, ambitions, will, and skill that made it possible for humans to fulfill this magnificent dream.

Below: **Lower Manhattan**, *where the* **East River** *and the* **Hudson River** *meet at the harbor.*

in Manhattan

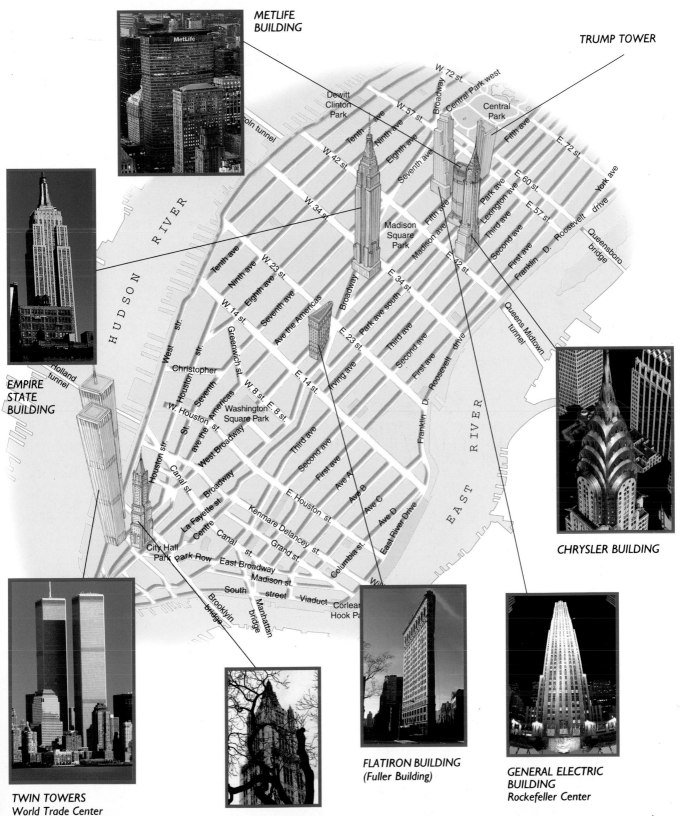

METLIFE BUILDING

TRUMP TOWER

EMPIRE STATE BUILDING

CHRYSLER BUILDING

TWIN TOWERS
World Trade Center
before the terrorist attack of
September 11, 2001

WOOLWORTH BUILDING

FLATIRON BUILDING
(Fuller Building)

GENERAL ELECTRIC BUILDING
Rockefeller Center

Twin Towers

The impressive Twin Towers, at the southern tip of Manahattan Island between Vesey and Liberty Streets and West and Church Streets, were the pride of one of the world's largest business complexes: the World Trade Center. The idea developed in the early 1960's as part of a plan to relaunch the downtown area as an international business and financial center; in fact, the New York Stock Exchange was also originally slated to move there.

The backers reviewed hundreds of plans before they selected Minoru Yamasaki and Emery Roth as architects; actual construction work began in 1969. The Towers were built of 185,000 tons of steel; the parts were prefabricated in the Midwest US and lifted into place by eight specially-built cranes brought in from Australia. The towers of the World Trade Center opened on April 4, 1973. The 1WTC tower soared to a height of 1709 feet (521 m) with its television antenna; its twin, 2WTC to 1362 feet (415 m). Both stood on foundations sunk to a depth of 755 feet (23 m). Although the towers were not very interesting from a stylistic standpoint, they opened equipped with a state-of-the-art telecommunications system comprising the first fiberoptic

The Winter Garden

Before the disaster of September 11, 2001, the spectacular Winter Garden in the World Financial Center, adjacent to the World Trade Center, was linked to it by an elegant covered elevated passageway. The view of the Hudson River and Ellis Island from this glass and steel building was magnificent. Its high nave hosted a palm grove that served as a garden setting for the cafes, restaurants, and bookstores that surrounded it, while the unconventional semicircular staircase in red and grey marble was used as an amphitheater for many events staged in this fascinating corner of New York.

*The two parallel piped towers of steel and glass that were the **Twin Towers** soared heavenward over the lower tip of Manhattan and for years were an essential feature of the city skyline.*

audiovisual network for commercial use ever installed in the United States. The observatory on the top floor of 1 WTC offered the city's most intoxicating view of New York and the Hudson River, with Staten Island, Ellis Island, and the Statue of Liberty. The famous "Windows on the World" restaurant and cocktail lounge—one of the city's most elegant spots—was located on the 107th floor.

The Birth of the Skyscrapers

*In 1950 an **antenna**, used for radio broadcasts, was added to the **tower**, bringing the total height of the Empire State Building to 1,454 feet (443.2 meters).*

***Pyramidal structures** made it possible to build tall buildings that would not block off light and avoid generating strong winds at street level.*

The first buildings of this type appeared on the skyline in the late 1800's, the years of New York's first business and industrial boom. That period also marked the beginning of a series of determinant technological innovations such as the invention of the elevator, industrial steel-making, and the development of fire-proof materials.

The 13-story Tower Building that was opened in 1888 is considered the first skyscraper ever raised in New York. In architectural terms these early buildings were inspired by styles of the past such as neo-Gothic or neoclassical. The finest examples from this period are the Flatiron Building and the monumental Woolworth Building that contemporaries nicknamed the "cathedral of commerce." Soon the people realized that the skyscrapers were blocking out considerable amounts of light from the nearby buildings and were creating strong air currents on the streets below. For this reason in 1916 New York passed zoning regulations that forced builders to decrease the constructed surface area as the buildings rose in height, and this led to the advent of the pyramid skyscraper. At the time real estate and construction were considered excellent investments, especially in New York where growth seemed unstoppable. The residential areas spread horizontally, expanding the city's boundaries towards the suburbs, while the vertical growth of the downtown business districts was about to change the city's skyline. In 1929 there were already 188 skyscrapers in New York. By the end of the Thirties, the first signs of market saturation began to be felt: the supply of business space definitely exceeded the demand.

During the third decade of the century, the United States was enjoying a period of such extraordinary economic growth that the era was dubbed "the roaring Twenties." Starting in those Twenties, Art Déco and the Bauhaus made themselves felt to the point of giving rise to two outstanding structures: the Chrysler Building and the Empire State Building. The modernist style gained strength during the following decade and flourished after World War II with the International movement. The linear shapes and motifs, along with the use of glass curtain walls distinguish many buildings of this period, the United Nations Building, the Twin Towers of the World Trade Center, and the Pan Am Building. Postmodernism came onto the scene in the Eighties, and in architecture this led to the neo-Modernist and Deconstructivist movements. By reacting to what had become a banal style architects designed original buildings that reinterpreted and combined motifs from previous eras. The Trump Tower is one example: the use of glass and straight lines recall the International style, but the original diagonal, staggered perimeters are a distinctive feature of contemporary decorativist architecture.

The Elevator

Skyscrapers could not exist if someone had not invented the elevator. The first steam-powered elevator was developed by Elisha Otis in 1852. Five years later the E.G. Otis company installed the first commercial passenger elevator in a New York department store. By 1873 there were over 2000 elevators operating in the United States. In the coming years Otis developed the hydraulic elevator that was less expensive and more efficient than the steam powered version. 1889 was the year of the first electric elevator that became semi-automatic in 1924, stopping at the requested floors without an operator.

The fully automatic elevator came into being in 1948, while in 1982, thanks to variable frequency technology, acceleration and stopping became more gradual. The latest innovation came in 1996 with the revolutionary Odyssey system that permits both vertical and horizontal movement so that the cabs can occupy the same shaft, opening the doors to a new generation of elevators.

The exploits of the men who built the **Empire State Building**, *in* **Lewis Wickes Hine**'s *photographs.*

© Collection of The New-York Historical Society (Negative Number 58337)

Cowboys in the Sky

"Like little spiders they toiled, spinning a fabric of steel against the sky" (*The New Yorker*).

An average of 3000 men, skilled and unskilled, worked at the Empire State Building construction site every day. Lewis Wickes Hines' famous pictures documenting the work can certainly be considered masterpieces of 20th century social photography.

The pictures of the welders' acrobatics as they nonchalantly hung in the air, hundreds of feet above ground, to position and weld the steel beams have gone down in history.

Every week, these welders assembled an average of 2400 tons of steel and managed to complete their contract in just six months.

Empire State Building

*The **Empire State Building** stands in the heart of Manhattan, on Fifth Avenue between 33rd and 34th Streets.*

Located between 33rd and 34th Streets, between Broadway and Fifth Avenue, the Empire State Building is in the heart of New York's business district. Extending over an area of nearly 79,000 square feet (7340 square meters) it covers the entire block. The address, 350 Fifth Avenue, was famous even before this masterpiece of modern architecture was erected. It was the site of the Waldorf Astoria, the hotel that made an era as the meeting place for society, politicians, and businessmen. In the Thirties the hotel moved to its current Park Avenue address, but before that it was the home of Caroline Schermerhorn Astor whose "Four Hundred Ball" was the highlight of the New York social calendar during the *Belle Époque*. Nearby is Macy's, built in 1902, the internationally famed store that is still operating the world's first escalator that is built entirely from wood. The other nearby attractions are Madison Square Garden (32nd Street and 7th Avenue) the famous sports arena, the Church of St. John the Baptist (34th Street and Broadway) with the magnificent tabernacle by Napoleon Le Brun, and the General Post Office (33rd Street and 8th Avenue), one of the finest examples of neoclassical—known as Beaux Arts—architecture the city has to offer that is open 24 hours a day.

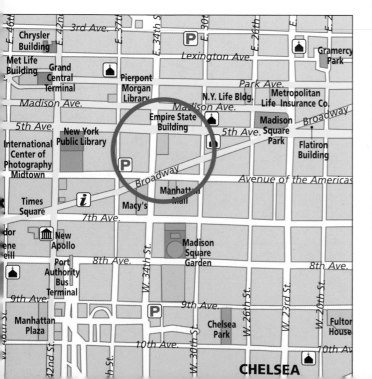

*On pages 36 and 37, a view of **Manhattan** looking north, with **Central Park** clearly visible in the near background.*

Zoom on the Empire

Even though it religuished its more than forty-year hold on the "world's tallest building" title in 1972, the Empire State Building still holds some impressive—and unsurpassed—records. From the artistic standpoint, it was the first American skyscraper to assimilate the lesson of the modernist school that had been launched in Europe by the Bauhaus. The simplicity of design and the harmony of its various elements confer unsurpassed subdued elegance. The recesses on the façades, for example, not only augment the dramatic effects of shadow and depth, they also increase the number of corner offices that are preferred because they have better lighting. The Empire State Building was also the first building to have visible, chrome-plated metal risers that serve both structural and decorative purposes, emphasizing the vertical grace. This technique, which permitted a marked reduction in the structure's specific weight, is considered a revolutionary architectural innovation.

Even the interior design was marked by several significant "novelties" such as the use of semi-permanent dividing walls that made it possible to offer tenants custom-sized offices; placing the radiators below the windows in the niches created by the sills, saving space and concealing them at the same time; and finally, the central position

A 204-foot (62-meter) television antenna was erected in 1950.

The soaring tower was developed to anchor dirigibles.

The observation decks are famous for the amazing view of the city.
Ever since it was built, the observation decks have been the secret of the building's fame and fortune, as they draw an endless stream of visitors. Actually, the original plans only called for one observation deck on the 86th floor, which was to be the top of the building. When the tower was added, another was created on the 102nd floor.

The exterior surface of the skyscraper is dotted by 6,500 windows.
An impressive number that gives the Empire State Building a particularly luminous face, a face that becomes even more dazzling and impressive when the colored spotlights on the top thirty stories are lit. There is a specific color for each holiday and celebration.

The Empire State Building has 73 elevators and they travel at top speed.
Passenger and freight elevators travel 1312 feet (400 meters) per minute and are indispensable to the daily life of the Empire State Building.

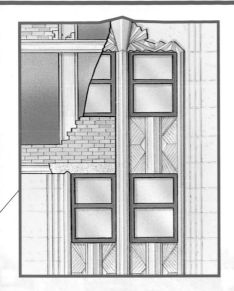

The use of prefabricated components made it possible to erect the Empire State Building in record time.

The skyscraper grew at the vertiginous rate of four stories a week. The facing was brick, while the windows were framed with steel panels; steel was also the material used for the decorative elements.

of the elevator shaft made available the maximum of usable floor space. From the engineering standpoint this skyscraper was the first building ever erected from prefabricated, standard-size components such as beams, pillars, and windows that were assembled on site. It was this system that made it possible to put up the building in record time: about four and a half stories per week! Work was organized with maximum efficiency—it was an assembly line operation. A rail transport system was built on each floor to distribute materials quickly and with a minimum effort: the trucks were unloaded in the basement, directly onto the elevators that carried the supplies to their destination.

Construction was a real show for New Yorkers. Every day a fascinated crowd would gather to watch the extraordinary, bustling progress of the works and mainly the breathtaking acrobatics of the workers suspended hundreds of feet above ground.

Lewis Hines' famous photographs document this event that was epoch-making for the city and its people. The work of over 3,000 men was coordinated with utmost precision and the contractors were selected for the quality of their products and their ability to meet deadlines. It was thanks to this efficient logistical organization that the Empire State Building could be completed in one year and 45 days, one month ahead of schedule. Therefore, the Empire State Building can justly be considered a masterpiece of beauty and efficiency.

*1930: **workers at dizzying heights** positioning a heavy slab during **construction** of the Empire State Building.*

© Collection of The New-York Historical Society (Negative Number 67435)

Technical Notes

Entrances: 5 on 33rd St., 5th Ave. and 34th St.
Total height: 1,454 feet (443.2 meters)
Antenna height: 204 feet (62 meters)
Floors: 102
Steps: 1860
Windows: 6500
Occupied floor space:
Area of site 79,288 square feet (7,340 square meters)
Weight: 365,000 tons

Weight of steel reinforcements: 60,000 tons (completed in 23 weeks)
Foundation supports: 200 steel and cement pylons
Facing: 10 million bricks
Foundation depth: 525 feet (16.7 meters)
Elevators: 73 (able to travel 1,181 feet/360 meters per minute)
Observatories: 2 (86th and 102nd floors)
Maintenance staff: 150

Chrysler Building

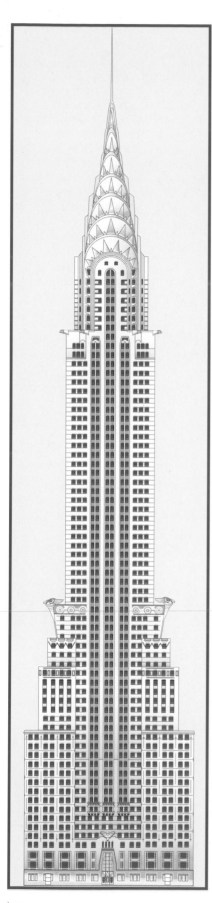

*The steel spire and distinctive architecture make the **Chrysler Building** one of the city's symbols.*

The Chrysler building is certainly one of the world's most recognizable skyscrapers with its steel Art Déco crown. Constructed in 1930, this 77-story building is located at 405 Lexington Avenue at 42nd Street and soars to a height 1,130 feet (319 meters). The project was initially started by former senator William J. Reynolds and was then taken over by Walter P. Chrysler of the automobile company. Like many magnates of the period who got involved in this type of project, Walter Chrysler was essentially motivated by the prestige that the tallest building in the world would confer on his name and business. The design by the New York architect William Van Alen was therefore modified several times so that Chrysler could obtain this record. Shortly before work was completed, Van Alen played his trump card and a 184 feet (56 meter) tall spire that had been constructed in great secrecy in the yard was hoisted above the cupola in 90 minutes. It was, however, a short-lived victory since the record was broken by the Empire State Building just a few months later.

The striking steel cupola by Nirosta is certainly the most fascinating element of this building. The stainless steel facing was arranged in rays with numerous triangular windows that follow the seven concentric parabolic curves on the four sides of the cupola.

The building's façades are much less original with black, white, and grey Oriental-style motifs. On Chrysler's request Van Alen added decorations that symbolize the automaker, such as stylized cars and another inspired by wheel rims, while the recesses on the upper floors were embellished with steel eagles whose wings are the logo of the company, and a few mock spouts in Gothic style. Unfortunately, these ornamental motifs are barely visible from street level, and even the base and entrance to the building can readily pass unobserved. The interiors, however, are extraordinary and have been restored to their original glory by the restructuring work done by the new proprietors in 1999. The entrance walls are faced with sumptuous red Moroccan marble, while the floor is made of yellow Siena marble with an amber

William Van Alen

William Van Alen (1883-1954) began studying architecture at the Pratt Institute in Brooklyn, where he was born. In 1908 he won a scholarship that allowed him to attend the École des Beaux Arts in Paris. He returned to New York in 1911 where he opened a studio with H. Craig Severance. Soon the two made a name for themselves with their innovative styles, especially in multi-story commercial buildings.

In 1925 Van Alen struck out on his own and four years later began working on the plans for the Chrysler Building. Even though this building is one of the masterpieces of Art Déco architecture, when the work was finally completed Walter Chrysler refused to pay him, accusing him of fraud and collusion with some contractors.

The architect appealed, but the suit was soon dropped. Even today, no one knows whether he was ever paid. Van Alen continued working, but because of the accusations launched by his client coupled with the Great Depression, he never had another opportunity to work on a project as prestigious as the Chrysler Building.

*In 1930 the **Chrysler Building** broke the height record held by the Woolworth Building, but not even one year later a new record was made by the Empire State Building, which became the protagonist of the New York panorama.*

and blue frame. The ceiling is covered with an enormous mural by Edward Turnbull entitled *Energy, Result, Workmanship and Transportation*.

Other noteworthy points are the elevators: the fine, carved wooden doors are considered Art Déco masterpieces. The staircase, with the magnificent chromed-plated balustrade leading to the mezzanine and basement, is also made in the same style. The observation deck below the spire is another spectacular portion of the Chrysler building, with its triangular windows that are tilted inwards. Unfortunately the observatory has been closed to the public for years.

Flatiron Building

*The 285-foot (87-meter) of the **Flatiron Building**, at 23rd Street where Fifth Avenue crosses Broadway, was built in 1902.*

Even though it was never the tallest skyscraper in the world, the Flatiron Building is certainly one of the most original and most photographed buildings in the world. Its triangular contour at the intersection of Fifth Avenue and Broadway at 23rd Street is one of the symbols of the city. Built in 1902 as the headquarters of the Fuller Construction Company, it rises 285 feet (87 meters) and is considered New York's oldest skyscraper. Originally it was known as the "Fuller Building," but the people constantly called it "Flatiron" so the nickname became the official name.

The plans were prepared by Daniel H. Burnham who had already achieved a certain amount of fame for other skyscrapers in Chicago.

From the engineering standpoint, the building immediately stood out as one of the most modern in New York since it had an independent electric heating system. For the exterior Burnham drew his inspiration from the Italian Renaissance. The idea was to make it resemble a very tall

classic column with a capital through plays of perspective. Therefore, it was built according to traditional architectural canons with a ground floor of shops, developing through the central stories, and concluding with an elaborate cornice above the 21st story.

Daniel Hudson Burnham

Daniel H. Burnham (1846-1912) is considered one of the major architects and city planners in America at the turn of the 20th century. Today, four of the skyscrapers he designed on his own (the Flatiron, New York) or with his partner John Wellbron Root (the Rookery, the Reliance Building and the Monadnock Building in Chicago) are national landmarks. The urban layout of Chicago in the last decade of the 19th century, considered to be thirty years ahead of its time, was widely imitated in other large American cities.

As opposed to other architects of the era, Burnham did not study at any prestigious European art school: after he finished his secondary education he went to work as an apprentice for the architects Carter, Drake and Wight. In 1873 he left to open a studio with Root, and soon specialized in steel skyscrapers. In 1881, the year his partner died, he was awarded the contract to design the World Columbian Exposition of 1893 that laid the foundations, as it were, for Chicago's urban development. The other famous buildings he designed include Selfridges's Department store in London (1909) and Union Station in Washington D.C. (1909).

Actually, Burnham succeeded so well that at first New Yorkers refused to visit the building because they were afraid it would fall over because of the strong winds at that intersection. But, if the gusts of wind never made it fall, they did contribute to its popularity.
Hordes of men would stand around the apex of the building hoping to catch of glimpse of ankles as the wind raised the skirts of the ladies who strolled by.

MetLife Building

*On these pages, the **MetLife** (formerly PanAm) **Building** by night, day, and in detail.*

The MetLife Building, originally known as the Pan Am Building, is one of New York's most controversial skyscrapers. Its bulk not only breaks the view of Park Avenue, the most elegant street in Manhattan, but it also blocks the classic beauty of Grand Central Terminal. Notwithstanding these criticisms, this 1963 building located at 200 Park Avenue at 45th Street is one of the city's finest examples of the International style. The project was originally awarded to Emery Roth who was joined by Walter Gropius and Pietro Belluschi as consultants. Gropius raised the height to 59 stories (807 feet - 246 meters) and conceived an octagonal base so that the building resembled the wing of an airplane, perfect for the main tenant, Pan American Airlines. The glass, cement, and granite façade is enlivened by two colonnades at the 21st and 46th floors, while the lobby is decorated with artworks such as the mural by Joseph Albers and the metal cable installation entitled *Flight*, by Richard Lippol. The lobby is connected to the railroad terminal by a series of covered passages.

In 1981 Pan Am sold the building to the MetLife insurance company, which changed its name.

Grand Central Terminal

Grand Central Terminal is unique in the world, from both the architectural and social standpoints. Not only is it unanimously considered a masterpiece of American architecture, but every day over 400,000 people go through it, creating a fascinating weave of lives and events. Built between 1903 and 1913, Grand Central Terminal combines of Beaux Arts Eclecticism of grandiose yet elegant and harmonious proportions with innovative engineering that makes it possible handle the enormous daily flow of passenger and train traffic. The main lobby and ticket office never cease to astound anyone who has seen Paul Helleu's fresco of the constellations that shine down from the vaulted ceiling. A recent restructuring project resulted in the creation of a lively mall with luxury boutiques and a huge variety of fast-food stores between the ground floor and under-ground level.

Trump Tower

Completed in 1983, the Trump Tower is located at 725 Fifth Avenue in the most elegant part of Midtown Manhattan; it is named for the builder and owner, Donald Trump. Designed by the architect Der Scurr of Swanke, Hayden, Connel & Co., this 68-story skyscraper (657 feet – 202 meters) is one of the most interesting examples of the first phase of the postmodern style. The classic parallelepiped with dark glass windows is enlivened by a diagonal cut on the corner of 5th Avenue and 56th Street. On that side the building rises with vertical and horizontal terraces that are decorated with ornamental plants. This is truly a multipurpose skyscraper: between the ground and sixth floors there are stores and restaurants, between the 7th and 20th are offices, and the remaining forty stories are home to 266 luxury apartments that are leased to tenants such as Sophia Loren and Johnny Carson. The lobby is lavishly decorated with red marble, mirrors, and shining brass in the opulent style of the Eighties. The main attraction is definitely the five-story high waterfall that dominates the main entrance of the shopping area.

*Two images of the **Trump International Hotel & Tower**.*

*Opposite, the **Trump Tower**: Donald Trump's midtown Tower has become a symbol of the yuppie generation.*

Donald Trump and His Empire

A true New Yorker from Queens, Donald Trump was certainly the most famous developer in the United States in the Eighties and Nineties thanks to a series of lucky deals and his passion for beautiful women. His first big real estate deal dates from 1976 when he purchased the neglected Commodore Hotel next to Grand Central Station and transformed it into an elegant—and profitable—concern.

The **Trump Tower**, where he maintains his offices and home—a 53-room penthouse—is his second prestigious undertaking. Between the Eighties and Nineties the Trump empire was growing at dizzying speeds, and not only in the field of luxury real estate in New York and Atlantic City, the Las Vegas of the East Coast. It also expanded to sports (he bought a New Jersey football team), an airline, a modeling agency, and a construction company. At the beginning of the Nineties the recession put a stop to this growth and Trump was forced to relinquish some prestigious properties such as the Plaza Hotel in New York.

In 1997 he completed the **Trump International Hotel & Tower**, a luxurious hotel and commercial building next to Central Park, while his most recent project is the Trump World tower, the world's tallest residential building.

Woolworth Building

*In 1913 neo-Gothic **Woolworth Building** was the tallest building ever erected, and it held the record until 1930.*

Considered by many to be the most beautiful commercial building in the world—it was nicknamed the "cathedral of commerce"—this skyscraper, designed by the architect Cass Gilbert is in fact a masterpiece of the neo-Gothic style that was in vogue in the United States at the beginning of the 20th century. Erected in 1913 at 223 Broadway, the Woolworth Building reaches a height of 729 feet and maintained its primacy as the world's tallest until 1930. Frank Woolworth, founder of the famous chain store, paid 13.5 million dollars in cash, thus launching a race among the magnates of the period that would continue throughout the Twenties. The building comprises a 27-story body and a 60-story tower on Broadway. Gargoyles, arches, and swirls follow each other on the façades that were restored to their original splendor in 1980—the restoration work cost more than construction! If the opulence of the exterior does not fail to arouse the admiration and wonder of anyone passing nearby, the interior is no less striking. The lobby is definitely one of the most lavish and elegant in New York. The vaulted ceilings are clad with mosaics as brilliant and sparkling as jewels and intricate, yet delicate, wrought iron and bronze ornaments abound.

The lobby is also decorated with bronze sculptures, one of which portrays Frank Woolworth counting the "nickels and dimes" on which he built his fortune.

The Nickel n'Dime Empire

Born in 1852 at Rodman New York, Frank Winfield Woolworth is the classic example of the self-made man who built an immense fortune out of nothing in the New World. Son of poor farmers, at his death Woolworth left a personal fortune of 65 million dollars. He began his career as a stock-boy in a store when he was twenty.

In 1879, after having heard about the success of selling items priced at 5 cents from a peddler, he convinced his employer to lend him a little less than $400 to open the first store where everything cost one nickel (5 cents).

The beginning was not easy, but Woolworth did not give up and in the end he managed to find the right places and products for his stores. Business took off after the recession of 1893 and Woolworth began opening his stores in the big cities such as Washington, Boston, and Philadelphia. His dreams were crowned by the opening of a large store in Manhattan in 1896 where there was even an organ. In 1897 he contacted the architect Cass Gilbert to build his corporate headquarters downtown. When Gilbert asked him how tall the building should be he answered, "750 feet." "You mean that is my limit?" asked the architect—to which the magnate replied, "No, that is the minimum."

World War I caused Woolworth some problems since he imported much merchandise from Europe, but it did not stop the growth of his chain that reached as far as Great Britain.

Woolworth died in 1919 of a tooth infection that he stubbornly refused to have treated.

G.E. Building

Originally known as the RCA (Radio Corporation of America) Building, the General Electric Building, at 850 feet (259 meters), is the tallest edifice in Rockefeller Center. Completed in 1933, this Art Déco structure is the culmination of several lessons learned during the construction of the Empire State Building, which it does not resemble even in the slightest. First of all the façade is made of Indiana limestone and its vertical sweep is achieved by the alignment of the windows. Even the interior was designed so that natural light could reach all the leasable floor space, maximizing its value. But even if the exterior is not particularly interesting, extreme care went into the design of the interior. The Art Déco ornamentation was inspired by classical mythology and the Rockefellers used the services of a philosopher to conceptualize the decorative theme. In the niche above the main entrance is the famous relief sculpture *Genius* by Lee Lawrie, while the walls are covered with murals by José Mari Sert. Opposite the building is the large, sunken Rockefeller Plaza that has been a luxurious ice skating rink since 1936 in winter and an elegant outdoor café in summer. The bronze statue of *Prometheus* by Paul Manship adorns the large fountain.

*Rockefeller Center, completed in 1940, rises around the 850-foot (259-meter) Art Déco **GE Building**.*

Radio City Music Hall

Rockefeller Center is the home of Radio City Music Hall, an institution in the New York world of entertainment. Since 1936, the year it was opened, to today over 300 million people have attended shows in this 6,200 seat theater that is still the largest and best equipped indoor theater anywhere in the world. The "Christmas Spectacular" show featuring the Rockettes is certainly the most famous, but even the rest of the calendar is filled with prestigious and high quality events. Part of the theater's long-lived success is due to the fabulous American Art Déco interior that ever since the beginning aroused such a sensation that one critic wrote, "It has been said of the new Music Hall that it needs no performers."
The designer Donald Desky, following the general theme "Human Achievement," created a tribute to the successes of the human race in the fields of the arts, science, and industry. All the interiors are original pieces made by Desky (or artisans he hired) using both traditional precious (gold leaf and marble) and industrial (bakelite, permatex and aluminum) materials.

Rockefeller Center and the Statue of Prometheus. In the summer, the plaza hosts the tables of the open-air restaurants; in the winter, it becomes the famous skating rink. The entrance from Fifth Avenue is decorated with flowers and plants.

Rockefeller Center

F rom Fifth Avenue to Avenue of the Americas (or 6th Avenue) and from West 47th Street to West 51st Street, the nineteen buildings and twenty-two acres (ca. 9 ha) that are Rockefeller Center constitute one of the most successful monuments to urban planning in the world. Rockefeller Center is really a city within a city, with its own fountains, gardens, promenades and thoroughfares, its own shops, commerce, and recreation. There are 15 million square feet (ca. 1.4 million sq m) of rentable space and a total daily population of 240,000. At first, however, the project seemed destined for failure.

With no small degree of hubris, John D. Rockefeller, Jr. conceived of the project as a means to extricate himself forever from the shadow of his father, Standard Oil baron John D. Rockefeller, Sr. With self-validation hanging in the balance, Rockefeller Jr. embarked on the titanic venture doggedly, paying $3.3 million for a twenty-four year lease on the land in 1928 and joining

RINK BAR
ROCKEFELLER CENTER

I BELIEVE IN THE SUPREME WORTH OF THE INDIVIDUAL
AND IN HIS RIGHT TO LIFE LIBERTY AND THE PURSUIT OF HAPPINESS

I BELIEVE
THAT EVERY RIGHT IMPLIES A RESPONSIBILITY· EVERY
OPPORTUNITY, AN OBLIGATION· EVERY POSSESSION, A DUTY

I BELIEVE
THAT THE LAW WAS MADE FOR MAN AND NOT MAN FOR THE
LAW· THAT GOVERNMENT IS THE SERVANT OF THE PEOPLE
AND NOT THEIR MASTER

I BELIEVE
IN THE DIGNITY OF LABOR, WHETHER WITH HEAD OR HAND·
THAT THE WORLD OWES NO MAN A LIVING BUT THAT IT
OWES EVERY MAN AN OPPORTUNITY TO MAKE A LIVING

I BELIEVE
IN THE SACREDNESS OF A PROMISE, THAT A MAN'S WORD
SHOULD BE AS GOOD AS HIS BOND, THAT CHARACTER—NOT
WEALTH OR POWER OR POSITION—IS OF SUPREME WORTH

I BELIEVE
THAT THE RENDERING OF USEFUL SERVICE IS THE COMMON
DUTY OF MANKIND AND THAT ONLY IN THE PURIFYING
OF SACRIFICE IS THE DROSS OF SELFISHNESS CONSUMED
AND THE GREATNESS OF THE HUMAN SOUL SET FREE

I BELIEVE
IN AN ALL-WISE AND ALL-LOVING GOD

BUSINESS OR PERSONAL AFFAIRS

I BELIEVE
TRUTH AND JUSTICE ARE FUNDAMENTAL TO AN
ENDURING SOCIAL ORDER

I BELIEVE
THAT LOVE IS THE GREATEST THING IN THE WORLD
THAT IT ALONE CAN OVERCOME HATE
THAT RIGHT CAN AND WILL TRIUMPH OVER MIGHT

JOHN D. ROCKEFELLER · JR

*The fountain outside the **Exxon Building** on 6th Avenue, facing **Radio City Music Hall**.*

*Radio City Music Hall** and the **G.E. Building** in Rockefeller Center.*

forces with the Metropolitan Opera, which was then looking for a new home. On October 29, 1929, the very day that architect Harvey Wiley Corbett was selected to direct the project, however, the stock market crashed. The Opera soon bowed out, and the Rockefellers were left with a staggering financial burden. Only Rockefeller's determination and his family's enormous wealth kept the project afloat. Not until years after World War II would Rockefeller Center emerge from out of the red and into the black.

Nevertheless, the show did go on. By 1940, 228 buildings had been razed and 4,000 people relocated to build the Center. Rockefeller's micro-city finally consisted of fourteen buildings, including the RCA Building, home of the National Broadcasting Company, and the Radio City Music Hall, then the world's largest indoor movie theater. In 1957 another five buildings were added, including the Time-Life Building. The main pedestrian entrance leads from Fifth Avenue through the Channel Gardens, lined with benches and greenery.

The famed Christmas tree and sunken skating rink are found in the heart of Rockefeller Plaza during the winter. In the spring the flower show arrives, and with the warm weather comes open-air dining. Or dine with a view from the sixty-fifth floor of the General

Electric Building—formerly the RCA Building—where the Rainbow Room offers superb vistas.

Rockefeller Center is impressively modern, artfully interpreting the grid and tower motif of its urban setting. The use of Art Déco brings a stylistic uniformity to Rockefeller Center, as does the use of Indiana limestone on all exterior surfaces. Architecturally, each building seems to bound upwards towards the heavens, the vertical planes creating a lofty aspect that adds to the sense of unity. As the centerpiece of the project, the G.E. Building conveys this towering ascendency most dramatically. One of the most incredible features of Rockefeller Center is the vast underground network of pedestrian tunnels and loading docks that keep over 700 delivery trucks out of sight every day.

Sculptures dot the landscape, including the impressive *Atlas Supporting the World* and the enormous gilded *Prometheus*. José Maria Sert's murals on the wall and ceiling of the G.E. Building lobby are worth checking out: they complement the Art Déco setting and, more importantly, pay homage to the spirit of capitalism that created Rockefeller Center. The original murals, begun by Diego Rivera in 1933, depicted a Homeric image of a valiant proletariat battling the forces of capitalist evil and, obviously, had to be painted over.

St. Patrick's Cathedral on 5th Avenue, across from *Rockefeller Center*, seen through the *Statue of Atlas*. Above, the Gothic-style interior of the cathedral.

St. Patrick's Cathedral

The largest Catholic church in the United States, St. Patrick's Cathedral is the seat of the Roman Catholic Archdiocese of New York and the spiritual home of the city's large Catholic population. Cramped in its urban setting across from Rockefeller Center, the cathedral is nevertheless considerably grand in scale, with 400 feet (ca.122 m) in length, 174 feet (53 m) in width and two towers each 330 feet (ca.100 m) in height. Designed by James Renwick, its construction began in 1858 and was not completed until 1879. Modeled on Germany's famed, much larger Cologne Cathedral, St. Pat's was conceived in a Gothic Revival style that includes French and English elements as well. The juxtaposition of the cathedral's sombre façade with its neighbors' glittering commercial storefronts is interesting, as are the bronze doors and masonry at the Fifth Avenue entrance. The interior, however, is even more impressive than the exterior. The nave is cavernous, with pews seating 2,500 people. Around the nave are a dozen altars, each dedicated to a different saint. The Lady Chapel, located behind the Italian-marble high altar, is exquisite. There is also a massive organ gallery, which belts out quite a large sound as well. The sixty or so stained-glass windows, including the lovely rose above the choir loft, are from Chartres, France.

Rockefeller Center's International Building seen through the Statue of Atlas.

Sports

N ew York is a city that does not
skimp on exciting sports.
Madison Square Garden is
famous worldwide for boxing matches
that made sports history. But even though
the championship bouts are now held in
Las Vegas and Atlantic City, the Garden
continues to be the venue for the
spectacular **NY Knicks** basketball games
and the **NY Rangers** hockey matches,
besides the stage for prestigious concerts.
New York also boasts two baseball
stadiums: **Shea Stadium** in Queens,
home of the **NY Mets,** and **Yankee
Stadium** in the Bronx, home of the **NY
Yankees.**
Strangely enough, New York has no
major-league football field, and the
NY Giants play their home games
across the river at **Giants Stadium** in
New Jersey.

The city is, however,
considering a number
of projects to bring the
home team back
home.
Another spectacular
New York sports event
is the **NY Marathon,**
held every year in the
early fall.

Yankee Stadium in
the Bronx and **Shea
Stadium** in Queens

*Boxing, baseball,
hockey, basketball,
the famous New York
Marathon: New York
offers many
occasions for
enjoying sports.*

Broadway:
Theater District and Times Square

The gaudy, vulgar spectacle of Times Square is for many around the world the ultimate symbol of New York City. The crowds, the horns, the towering advertisements, the blaze of flashing neon lights—there is something incredibly powerful at work here, at least for a first-time visitor. For better of for worse, this can at times feel like the center of the universe, especially on New Year's Eve.

Originally known as Longacre Square, this monumental crossroads changed to its present name in 1904, when the *New York Times* moved its headquarters to One Times Square. At midnight on December 31, 1904, the paper threw a fireworks celebration for itself, and the tradition has continued ever since. Hundreds of thousands of people flock to Times Square, with millions more watching on television world-wide, as the ball drops here to signify a new year.

With a glittering exuberance that rivals even Las Vegas, the spirit of Times Square hasn't changed much since its creation. While the *Times* has moved around the corner, it left its Motogram electronic headline sign wrapped around its former home at One Times Square. This beacon of light, along with Broadway's original blazing theater marquees, transformed the square: today all buildings are required by the city to devote a portion of their façades to illuminated advertisements. Beyond the pomp and glitz, of course, Times Square is also the country's premier showcase for theater. It has become the Mecca of the theater world, attracting over two million persons a year. Do note, however, that "Broadway theater" refers not to a geographic location but to a theatrical standard of production. A Broadway show is large-scale in every aspect, with cast and crew the size of small armies, spectacular set designs, and big-name stars. Times Square provides the space and the crowds for such grand productions.

Off-Broadway shows are smaller, with a minimum 100-seat audience capacity. Off-Off-Broadway is smaller yet, and often experimental in nature. Some of the grand old theaters are just now reviving. The historic New Amsterdam Theater was remodeled by the Disney Company, the New Victory by the Times Square Redevelopment organization. The two face each other on West 42nd Street, once a menacing thoroughfare of porn shops but now much more family oriented. The latest spectacular skyscraper facing onto this celebrated square is the Condé Nast Building, erected in 1999.

Broadway's stages have something for everybody — grandiose productions, serious theater, and scintillating musicals.

*On the follwing pages, some views of **Times Square** illuminated by its bright advertising signs and marquees.*

*On these pages, views of **Central Park**, the most important green space in Manhattan, in the **Uptown** area.*

The boulevards created for horse-drawn carriage traffic are now the dominion of joggers and cyclists.

Central Park

The lush stomping ground for 15 million New Yorkers and tourists every year, Central Park literally transformed the landscape of cities around the world by setting a new standard for urban open spaces. There are now over a hundred monuments, besides the Metropolitan Museum of Art on 14 acres (5.7 ha) of the park's east side, and the American Museum of Natural History (west side). In the wintertime the place to be for ice-skating is **Wollman Rink.** Once a pasture where cows from the nearby former Dairy used to graze, the rink was opened by Donald Trump—with great publicity —when the city was unable to supply the necessary funds. Considerable acclaim was also heaped on the **Central Park Zoo** when it reopened in 1988 after being closed for several years. This progressively managed zoo tries to provide its inhabitants with an environment as similar as possible to their habitat in the wild. Larger animals, therefore, are not included. As always, the main attraction here is the sea lion pool. Just east of **Sheep Meadow**—a great place to lounge in the summertime—**The Mall** is architecturally the most formal element from the original mid-1800's

Greensword Plan by Frederick Law Olmsted and Calvert Vaux. The centerpiece is **Bethesda Fountain**, built in 1863 to commemorate those who died at sea during the Civil War. **Strawberry Fields** was sponsored by Yoko Ono as an international garden of peace. Ono's husband, John Lennon, was slain near the spot in 1980. A large mosaic that reads "Imagine" is set into the sidewalk, and the plants were donated by countries from all around the world. Further north is **Belvedere Castle**, designed by Vaux as an original feature of the park and now home to the Urban Park Rangers Meteorological Station and Learning Center—and a useful backdrop for Shakespearean dramas performed nearby at the **Delacorte Theatre**. A gift to the city from George Delacorte, the venue offers free tickets for the Shakespeare Festival held every summer.

Cleopatra's Needle was installed in 1877. According to some, New York would join the ranks of the world's great cities only when it erected its first Egyptian obelisk. Khedive Ishmail Pasha of Egypt obliged by presenting the City of New York with this 16th-century BC obelisk commemorating the achievements of King Thutmose.

*Facing page, a view of **Central Park**.*
*On this page, images from the **Intrepid Sea-Air-Space Museum**,*
the world's largest naval museum, on the Hudson River.

On the following pages:
*the crowded steps of the **New York Public Library** at the corner*
of 42nd Street and 5th Avenue, one of the stone lions at the
*entrance, and a detail of the **pediment**; the **Lincoln Center for**
***the Performing Arts** on Columbus Avenue between West 62nd*
and West 65th Streets.

Intrepid Sea-Air-Space Museum

T he Intrepid Sea-Air-Space Museum consists of three decommissioned U.S. military vessels docked along the piers at West 46th Street on the Hudson River: the *Intrepid*, a World War II aircraft carrier; the *Growler*, a nuclear missile submarine; and the *Edson*, a Vietnam-era destroyer. The centerpiece of the Museum, of course, is the *Intrepid*, an immense flattop that houses over forty aircraft and other military vehicles on its decks. Among the arsenal are a Stealth bomber, an Iraqi tank captured in the Gulf War, a Russian guided missile and other assorted space capsules, rockets and missiles. Besides its enormity—the *Intrepid* spans over 900 feet (almost 275 m)—the ship has a storied past that includes having spearheaded the defeat of the Japanese navy in the Fall of 1944 and later almost being sunk by Japanese kamikaze pilots.

New York Public Library

The New York Public Library system boasts 82 branches and 7 million users annually. The central library alone has 92 miles (148 km) of computerized stacks and over 3 million books.

The grand Beaux-Arts building that houses it was completed in 1911 and stands as a white marble temple to the pursuits of reason, education, and beauty with an exquisitely detailed colonnaded and pedimented façade. The monumental stairs to the entrance are flanked by two ornate flagpoles and a pair of fountains to Truth and Beauty. The two sculpted stone lions, christened Patience and Fortitude by Mayor Fiorello La Guardia, are the library's world-renowned gatekeepers.

Lincoln Center

One of the foremost cultural centers of the world, Lincoln Center is home to the Metropolitan Opera, the New York Philharmonic, the New York City Ballet, the New York City Opera, the Juilliard School of Music, the Film Society of Lincoln Center, and the Library and the Museum of the Performing Arts. The fourteen-acre (5.7 ha) complex was built between 1962 and 1968, at cost of $220 million. The project is certainly not without faults: one might even question the need to concentrate so many stalwart institutions in one space. For all these dilemmas, however, Lincoln Center is a powerful life-force in this city, and a cultural acropolis throughout the world.

The most distinctive building is the **Metropolitan Opera House**, designed by Wallace Harrison. The overall appearance is dominated by the five horseshoe-shaped proscenium arches. From outside at night, the Metropolitan appears quite impressive, with several massive Austrian crystal chandeliers burning brightly inside. Two huge, colorful Chagall tapestries hang in the lobby. The floors are covered in royal red carpet, and the stair railings are hammered brass. The four-tiered theater itself is luxurious, although not overly adorned. With great effect at the start of a performance, the chandelier overhead ascends to the ceiling. The stage affords wonderful large-scale productions—typically enhanced by a diva or two—with excellent acoustics and technological brilliance. The New York City Ballet also performs here.

Kitty-corner to the Metropolitan Opera is perhaps the most aesthetically pleasing edifice of the group, the **New York State Theater**, designed by Philip Johnson with a mirror motif inside and out. This is home to both the New York City Opera and the American Ballet Theater.

Opposite the New York State Theater is **Avery Fisher Hall**, residence of the New York Philharmonic as well as the Serious Fun and Mostly Mozart Festivals. Most seats here are in the vast orchestra, and the decor is effectively simple. The **Vivian Beaumont** and the much smaller **Mitzi Newhouse** Theaters both rise behind a reflecting pool where a Henry Moore sculpture is prominently featured. The Beaumont, a 1,100 seat Broadway venue, was designed by Eero Saarinen and is perhaps Lincoln Center's most daring, if severe, piece of architecture. **Alice Tully Hall** presents an intimate setting for recitals and chamber music.

American Museum of Natural History

The American Museum of Natural History is one of the largest of its kind in the world. The museum takes up four square city blocks and houses more than thirty million objects. The museum complex consists of twenty-three interconnected buildings and forty galleries, which serve almost three million visitors per year. The museum's façade is an amalgam of architectural styles: while the central building and its offshoots have a robust classical style, the 77th Street entrance is Romanesque Revival. The main entrance, on Central Park West, features several interesting statues, including one of Rough Rider Teddy Roosevelt, a museum benefactor in his day. Frozen in pitched battle, a group of enormous dinosaur skeletons in the lobby quickly grabs one's attention. The drama here is captured in *medias res*, as a ferocious Allosaurus lunges to devour a mother and baby Barosaurus. Even after such a rousing introduction, the museum's other superb holdings are sure to impress. In the galleries beyond the lobby and on the second floor, dioramas recreate the natural habitats of a wide variety of animals. The animals are stuffed, of course, and the habitats painted, but there is a quirky charm in these displays, some of which are sixty years old. Among the highlights are dioramas of animals from the African jungles and the Sahara, as well as Asia and the North American plains. While many of the exhibits are highly scientific, it doesn't take a degree in paleontology to be wowed by the world's largest collection of dinosaur skeletons, located on the fourth floor. Some of these impressive beasts are 65 million years old and exceed 60 feet (18 m) in length. The museum also houses the IMAX Theater with a 60-foot-tall screen (18 m plus). The constantly changing films are dedicated, of course, to themes of natural history.

Rose Center for Earth and Space - This spectacular pavilion of the American Museum of Natural History, reopened in 2000, is home to the new **Hayden Planetarium** and the museum of astrophysical sciences. The new museum contains many interesting exhibits and a large theater where the feature attractions are the three-dimensional high-definition Digital Galaxy projections of all the heavenly bodies discovered to date, created in collaboration with the US NASA. The show leaves you breathless as you are "beamed up" to the most remote galaxies and nebulas in just a few seconds time—accompanied by the voice of Tom Hanks.

*The **American Museum of Natural History:** bottom left, Hall of Vertebrate Origins; bottom right, some of the many like-life animals in yhe wildlife dioramas; opposite, top: Hall of Saurischian Dinosaurs, Tyrannosaurus Rex; bottom: Theodore Roosevelt Rotunda and Hall of Advanced Mammals Mammoth.*

The Metropolitan Museum of Art

Without question, the Metropolitan Museum of Art ranks among the world's half-dozen or so greatest museums. Founded in 1870, it is the largest museum in the Western Hemisphere and houses well over 3 million objects of art, including the planet's largest collection of medieval artifacts. The original holdings consisted mainly of Cypriot antiquities and 170 Dutch and Flemish paintings acquired under the directorship of General Louis Palma de Cesnola. Suffice it to say that the museum has grown tremendously. The Metropolitan now has whole departments devoted to just about every conceivable artistic discipline: European Painting, Islamic Art, Ancient Near Eastern Art, Egyptian Art, Arms and Armor, European Sculpture and Decorative Arts, Medieval Art, Twentieth-century Art, Asian Art, Greek and Roman Art, the Art of Africa, the Americas and the Pacific Islands, Drawings, Prints, and Photographs. There's even a Musical Instruments section and a Costume Institute.

A tour of the museum typically begins with the **European Painting** galleries at the top of the grand staircase. The Dutch painters are well-represented, with Old Masters like Vermeer, Hals, Steen, Van Ruysdael, and Rembrandt leading the way. Take note, the Met's Dutch collection is probably the best to be found outside of the Netherlands. Among the most exquisite works are Vermeer's sublime *Young Woman with a Water Jug* and Rembrandt's sobering *Self-Portrait*. The Italians fare no worse here. Giotto's *Epiphany* grandly heralds the beginning of the Renaissance, with masterpieces by the likes of Giovanni Bellini, Filippo Lippi, Botticelli, Tintoretto, and Veronese soon to follow. Raphael's *Madonna and Child Enthroned with Saints* appears truly transcendent, while *Venus and the Lute Player,* one of many Titians on display, is all power.

Several masterworks by Rubens, including *A Forest at Dawn with a Deer Hunt* and a highly stylized self-portrait with his wife and son, suggest the ethereal quality of the Flemings. Not to be outdone, Van Eyck, Van der Weyden, and Van Dyck offer many opulent sylvan scenes and telling portraits done in minute detail.

The Spanish collection, if smaller in size, is nevertheless exquisite in scope. Few museums can claim a worthy challenge to the triumvirate of El Greco's apocalyptic *View of Toledo*, Velázquez's *Juan de Pareja,* and Goya's *Majas on a Balcony.* The Metropolitan is also home to an astounding collection of English portraits by Gainsborough, Thomas Lawrence, and Sir Joshua Reynolds, whose *Colonel George K. H. Coussmaker* presents an uncanny pose of casual but studied negligence.

Seventeenth-century French painting is well-represented

*The **Metropolitan Museum of Art**, on 5th Avenue between East 80th and East 84th Streets, is the largest city museum in the world, and is practically impossible to visit in a single trip.*
On the facing page, top, Two Tahitian Women *by Paul Gauguin and* Cypresses *by Vincent Van Gogh; bottom, Francisco Goya's* Don Manuel Manrique Osorio de Zuñiga *and* Flora *by Rembrandt.*

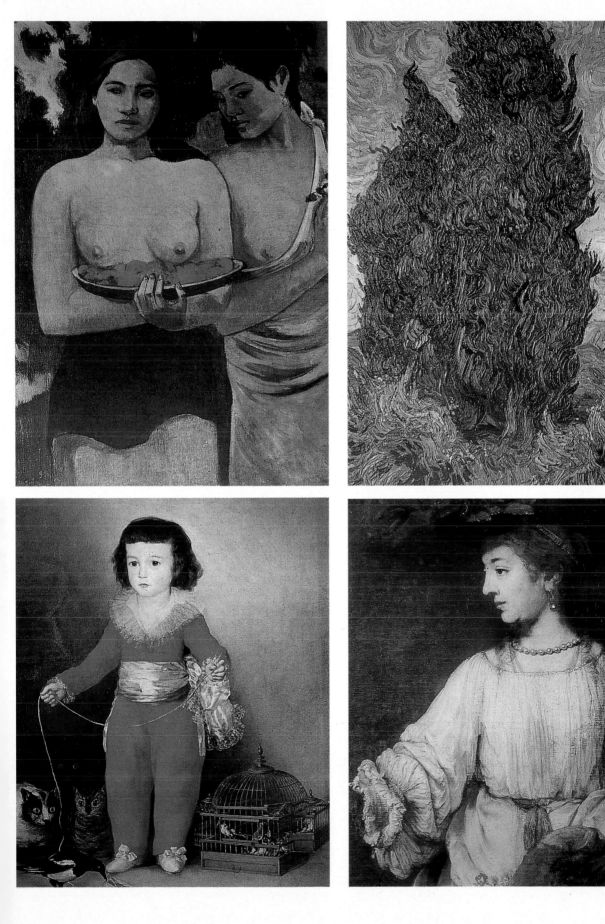

by Nicolas Poussin who, among others, serves his country well at the Metropolitan. *The Rape of the Sabine Women* attests not only to his profound knowledge of mythology and archaeology, but also to his rigorous skill of dramatic interpretation. The Met's Impressionist collection is well-stocked and includes all the big names: Cézanne, Pissarro, Manet, Degas, Monet, and Renoir in glorious abundance, Rousseau, Gauguin, Van Gogh, Toulouse-Lautrec, and Seurat, to name a few. Among the most influential works are Monet's *The Terrace at Sainte-Adresse*, Degas' *Dancers Practicing at the Bar*, Cézanne's *Rocks in the Forest*, and Van Gogh's *Cypresses*.

The **American Wings** house an unmatched collection of paintings, prints, drawings, furniture, and other decorative arts. Paintings include many seminal works in American history, like Ralph Earl's *Elijah Boardman*, Gilbert Stuart's *George Washington*, and Emanuel Gottlieb Leutze's *Washington Crossing the Delaware*. The pastoral, romantic vision of Thomas Cole's *View From Mount Holyoke* and Frederic Church's *Heart of the Andes* reflect the ideals of the Hudson River School, which shaped the first generation of American landscape artists. John Singer Sargent's *Madame X*, Mary Cassatt's *Lady at the Tea Table*, and Thomas Eakins' *Max Schmitt in a Single Scull* are the highlights from the American twentieth century.

On the main floor, the Metropolitan's **Egyptian collection** ranks among the world's best. The centerpiece of the collection is the *Temple of Dendur*, an 82-foot sandstone monument from the early Roman period (ca. 15 BC). Of course, the Metropolitan's **collection of ancient Near Eastern**, Greek, and Roman artifacts is superb, and well documents the origins of Western civilization. Among the intricately detailed funerary vases, urns and bowls that make the **Greek collection** noteworthy, perhaps the single most important and awe-inspiring object is the marble *Kouros* (ca. 610 BC). The Metropolitan claims to have the largest **collection of Islamic art** in the world, and by the looks of it, there's no reason to doubt it. The distinct histories of the three great **Asian civilizations**—those of India, China and Japan—are recorded in great detail at the Metropolitan.

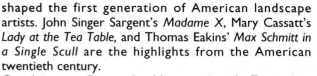

The collection shows how foreign invasions—both cultural and military—influenced the evolution of each civilization. The Metropolitan's **collection of African and Oceanic art** shows that these traditions are as old and complex as any in the world.

One of the museums newer wings is devoted to **Twentieth century art**. Picasso's exacting portrait *Gertrude Stein* speaks volumes on its subject. Matisse's *Nasturtiums with "Dance"* explores the power of color in the Fauvist tradition, while Hopper's *Lighthouse at Two Lights* is a seminal work in American objective painting. The fleshy corpulence of Lucian Freud's blunt *Back View of Nude* will give you a start, as will abstractions by Willem de Kooning, Jackson Pollock, and Barnett Newman.

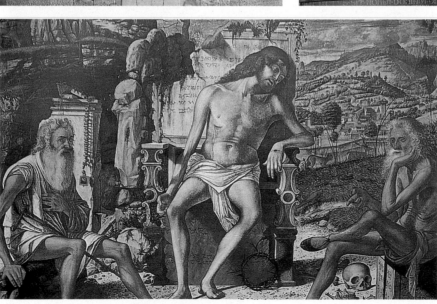

Metropolitan Museum of Art. Above, a detail of the Temple of Dendur (ca. 15 BC) reconstructed in the Egyptian section of the museum, and Guariento's Virgin and Child. *Below,* The Meditation on the Passion *by Vittore Carpaccio.*

*On the facing page, the **Guggenheim Museum** at the corner of 5th Avenue and East 89th Street.*

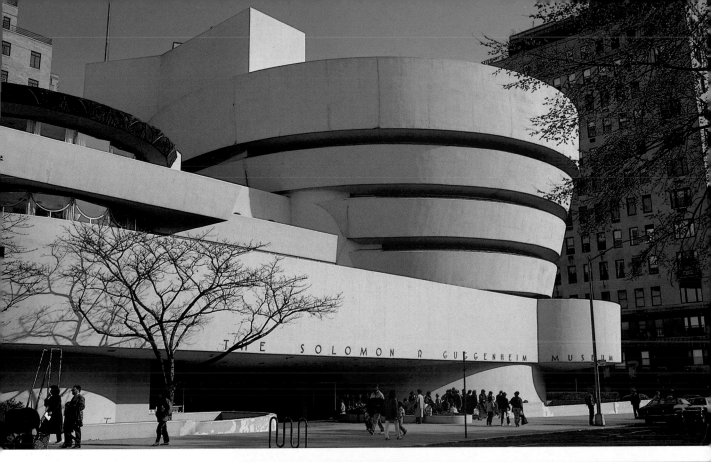

Solomon R. Guggenheim Museum

At least as famous for its spiraling architecture as for its modern art collection, the Guggenheim Museum is Frank Lloyd Wright's only building in New York City and represents quite a departure from his residential designs.

In the fashion of Le Corbusier, Wright considered his design to be organic, and therefore the building's overall circular motif is reflected in many intricate details.

The collection includes well over 3,000 works and is perhaps best known for its abstract art, which ranges from the fantasy of Kandinsky's *Small Pleasures* to the rigorous rationale of Mondrian's *Composition 2*, from the bluntness of Kline's *Painting No. 7* to the colorful, lyric harmony of Delaunay's *Simultaneous Windows*. The newest gallery, opened in 1993, contains several great works by figurative photographer Robert Mapplethorpe.

The Museum of Modern Art

The MoMA QNS builiding.

MoMA QNS - In the spring of 2002, the MoMA collections and exhibits moved to Long Island City, Queens, where they will stay until early 2005. The California architect Michael Maltzman designed the sensational makeover of the former warehouse that is the museum's temporary home. As you leave the 33rd Street elevated station of the No. 7 local subway train, the first thing you'll see is the roof of the new museum space, where the MoMA logo forms in huge letters in the style typical of the commercial premises and depots in the area. At street level, the path to the museum entrance is clearly identified by lighting and continues on into the entrance on a ramp that separates the ticket counter from the museum shop and snack bar. The ramp leads on into the exhibition space proper, which occupies two floors of the building.

The Museum of Modern Art and the MoMA collections - The Museum of Modern Art, or **MoMA** as it is commonly called, can rightly be considered THE modern art museum. In short, the MoMA is a repository of the history of modern art, with exhibits of what is to all effects a complete, representative collection of the art of the 20th century including some of its best and most innovative works. Besides in terms of simple numbers (more than 100,000 works and more than 1.5 million visitors annually), the MoMA has been decisive for the pioneer work it has carried out in the field of modern art since its inception more than 60 years ago. In the summer of 2002, the MoMA moved to Queens (**MoMA QNS**) where it will stay until early 2005 to make way for the renovation work underway at the 53rd Street museum

Pablo Picasso (1881-1973), Les Demoiselles d'Avignon, 1907.

building and construction of an adjacent extension designed by the architect Yoshio Taniguchi.

Three influential collectors of modern art, Abby Aldrich Rockefeller, Lillie Bliss, and Mrs. Cornelius J. Sullivan, generated the support necessary to found the institution in 1929. Under the guidance of director Alfred H. Barr Jr., the museum's inaugural exhibition featured works by Cézanne, Gauguin, Seurat and Van Gogh, and was followed in the next decade by two other groundbreaking exhibitions, *Cubism and Abstract Art* and *Fantastic Art, Dada, and Surrealism.* The profound influence of these shows quickly made MoMA the world's Mecca of modern art. It could be said that MoMA even helped define the parameters of modern art by creating its own departments: painting and sculpture, drawings, prints, photography, film, architecture, industrial and graphic design. This multidisciplinary approach to contemporary art has

been emphasized by special exhibitions — often iconoclast, or at least somewhat incendiary in nature — that range from an inimitable Matisse retrospective in 1992 to an intriguing study of the industrial design potential of Mutant Materials in 1995.

The 53rd Street building was constructed by Edward Durrell Stone and Philip Goodwin on the site of a Rockefeller family house in 1939, a decade after the museum was founded in rented rooms on Fifth Avenue. In 1964 Philip Johnson remodeled the museum and added the East Wing, and in 1984 Cesar Pelli designed the West wing, which, among other things, doubled the gallery space and enlarged the sculpture garden in back.

A tour of MoMA will invariably begin with the seminal works of the twentieth century, those that forever changed the ways in which we view art and, without doubt, the modern world. Around each corner, you'll see many old acquaintances, images that have grown up with the twentieth century.

The earliest works include those by the Impressionists and Post-Impressionists, among them Monet's large-scale triptych *Water Lilies*, Van Gogh's *Starry Night* and Cézanne's *Still Life with Apples*. The latter exemplifies an extraordinarily modern vision, one that greatly influenced the history of modern art. Despite appearances, the painting is not unfinished, but rather redefines notions of completeness. A rigorous and infinitely complex geometry binds the composition, foreshadowing the Cubist movement.

Matisse is another standout in the collection, which includes 36 of his works, several of which are sculptures. Among the most alluring paintings are *The Red Studio,* in which throbbing red tonalities push the limits of Fauvism, and *Dance*, a masterpiece depicting Matisse's elegant *joie de vivre*.

Picasso's *Les Demoiselles d'Avignon*, painted in 1907, is among the most important works in the history of modern art and represents, in many ways, the beginning of a new, truly modern artistic sensibility. The violent intensity of this painting obliterated all vestiges of what was then the vanguard of modern painting, Fauvism, and introduced the world to the first twentieth-century school of art, Cubism. Note the means of the painting:

Marc Chagall (1887-1985), I and the Village, *1928.*

Francis Bacon, (1909- 92), Second Version of a Painting from 1946.

the tendency to abstraction, the attack of the brush-work, the primitive geometry of human forms and space, the distorted and claustrophobic perspective. But note too the moral significance of the painting: the ferocity of the subjects' gazes, the way in which the viewer is brought into the scene, implicated in this harrowing narrative. Other notable works that demonstrate Picasso's vast range include earlier work such as *Boy Leading a Horse* and *Two Nudes*, and later works like *Girl Before a Mirror, Seated Bather* and *Three Musicians*.

The Cubism hinted at by *Les Demoiselles* is perfected shortly after by Georges Braque in *Man with a Guitar*. This conceptual means of painting is then adopted by such greats as Juan Gris in *Guitar and Flowers*, and even later by the Futurists, who used these structural devices to convey a love of power, movement and speed. Carlo Carrà's painting *Funeral of the Anarchist Galli*, Gino Severini's *Armored Train in Action* and Umberto Boccioni's bronze sculpture *Unique Forms of Continuity in Space* depict this violent vision. Constantin Brancusi's *Bird in*

Space, on the other hand, is fluid elegance, flight itself cast in bronze.

Of another world all-together is the intense and discomfiting German Expressionism rendered by the likes of Schiele, Kokoschka, Nolde and Kirchner. Max Beckmann's *Family Picture* captures the flavor of neurosis here with tragi-comic effect. Wassily Kandinsky's abstract *Picture with an Archer* and Marc Chagall's poetic, dreamy *Birthday* follow vaguely in these stylistic traditions, although infused with more than a touch of fantasy and folklore and rather less angst. In this very modern museum, none are more progressive-minded than the Dutch minimalist Piet Mondrian. MoMA lays claim to sixteen of his paintings, a survey of which demonstrates the evolution of a unique and highly-intellectual abstractionism. Mondrian continually reinvented himself as a painter, as his last completed painting, *Broadway Boogie Woogie*, shows. Here the purist's affinity for primary colors and rectilinear form is unyielding, yet at the same time a great departure. In this last year of his life, Mondrian's abstraction achieves an as-

pect of Impressionism, portraying New York City — brilliantly — in the pulsing neon and staccato rhythm of mere colored squares.

The enigmatic paintings of Giorgio de Chirico appeal to another level of consciousness entirely, anticipating Surrealist pursuits by over a decade. In *The Song of Love*, the juxtaposition of oneiric symbolism with the mundane creates a strangely off-putting composition, one that alludes to a metaphysical presence in the objective world. The works of Yves Tanguy, René Magritte, Paul Delvaux and Salvador Dali follow in that tradition.

Dali's *Persistence of Memory* also delves into the nether regions of the psyche, presenting a Freudian, dreamlike scenario of melting watches and a slumbering fetal creature set in a post-apocalyptic landscape. Later works such as Francis Bacon's *Dog*, for example, share this nightmarish quality and attest to the far-reaching influence of Surrealism.

Amid the abstractions and distortions of modern art, American Realism stands undaunted. Charles Sheeler's *American Landscape*, Edward Hopper's *House by the Railroad*, and Andrew Wyeth's *Christina's World* show how truly modern and provocative a realism can be.

MoMA holds no less than twenty-one exemplary works by Joan Miró. One of the largest, *The Birth of the World*, also happens to be one of the most important. Perhaps no other painting made before World War II so clearly anticipates the coming of Abstract Expressionism. The mix of improvisational painting techniques — haphazard spilling and blotting — with tightly controlled linear brushwork presents a vivid conflict. Miró creates his own universe here, as the title suggests, and this genesis becomes a metaphor for the act of artistic creation itself. All the major Abstract Expressionists are in attendance at MoMA: from Jackson Pollock and Willem de Kooning, to Philip Guston, Robert Motherwell and Franz Kline. In Pollock's frenzied *One*, poured, blotted, sprinkled and dripped paint all congeal in an intense maelstrom of color and movement. At the same time,

painters like Mark Rothko, Ad Reinhardt and Barnett Newman achieve a more sublime intensity exploring the depths of color fields.

Riding the crest of Abstract Expression, where anything goes, the likes of Roy Lichtenstein, James Rosenquist, Jasper Johns and, most famously, Andy Warhol create a Pop Art sensation in the late '50s and early '60s. John's *Flag* transformed the familiar stars-and-stripes image into an abstracted, painterly field, confounding the distinction between art and artlessness. So too does Warhol's *Gold Marilyn Monroe* push the limits of art, demanding the viewer to accept a banal, even profane subject matter as a sacred icon by shrouding the image in Byzantine-style gold. Beyond all the paintings and sculptures, there's still much more to see at MoMA.

A department is devoted to architecture and design, and displays range from models and renderings of outstanding contemporary buildings to chairs, lamps, a vacuum cleaner, a set of lobster forks, a chrome toaster and an already archaic turntable. The flashy red Cisitalia 202 GT was the first automobile to have entered any art museum in the world and symbolizes the museum's progressive vision. Like the rest of the MoMA collection, the photographs represent the best of the best. From ghostly albumen-silver prints to funky polaroids, it's worth a look. Finally, with all that behind you, you can catch your breath in the sculpture garden and sit among such outstanding works as Rodin's *Monument to Balzac*, Barnett Newman's 25-foot *Broken Obelisk*, Picasso's *She-Goat* and a quartet of bronze reliefs by Matisse.

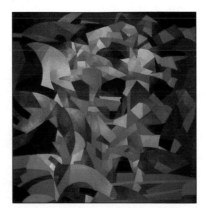

SoHo

The neighborhood's name is a contraction of its geographical position (SOuth of HOuston Street). It is no longer the slum district it once was, now being home to some of the city's most elegant boutiques, which in turn supplanted the many art galleries that before them toned up the area.

The first changes began in the 1960's, when an avant-garde of artists installed itself in the spacious (and low-rent) former warehouse lofts and shops of the neighborhood and radically transformed the atmosphere of what had been only a squalid low-rent housing and seedy business district. And as was to later happen in TriBeCa, the "Bohemian" atmosphere attracted the middle class and the world of finance, transforming SoHo—in just two decades—into a lively center for culture and inflating property prices out of all proportion.

SoHo is now mainly a mecca for shoppers, although there do remain a few galleries, museums, and spaces dedicated to the performing arts. One striking example among the victims of the new "invaders" is the **Guggenheim Museum SoHo**: the ground floor is now a Prada boutique, while the museum has been relegated to the upper stories.

The **New Museum of Contemporary Art**, on Broadway, includes a section dedicated to the digital arts. Even though many famous galleries (like the Holly Solomon and the Pace-Wildenstein) have moved to Chelsea, SoHo still hosts some of the most prestigious, like **Deitch Projects**, with its contemporary art specialization, and the **Howard Greenberg Gallery** of photography. One of the most fascinating parts of the area is the **SoHo Cast Iron Historical District**, comprised in the main between Houston Street, West Broadway, Crosby Street, and Canal Street, where—thanks to the generous donations of private citizens—a valid attempt has been made to conserve the cobbled streets and the beautiful cast-iron of the façades. The material, which offered the possibility of creating low-cost architectural decoration, was selected for this use by the iron magnate James Bogardus in the mid-19th century.

*The characteristic façades and the iron fire escapes of the buildings in **SoHo** and the **West** and **East Villages**.*

*The Arch in **Washington Square Park** marks the start of 5th Avenue in the center of **Greenwich Village**.*

Greenwich Village

Today **Washington Square Park** represents one of New York's most well-preserved melting pots. Originally a soupy marsh, the Square served as communal burial ground for some 20,000 cholera victims in the eighteenth and early nineteenth centuries. Later, and as late as 1819, the Square was the site of public executions. The large elm in the northwestern corner of the park—believed to be the oldest tree in Manhattan—served as hanging tree for many of New York's con-

demned villains. Washington Square became a public park on July 4, 1828.

The **Triumphal Arch** on the north side is the park's most prominent feature and was erected—in wood—to commemorate the centennial of George Washington's inauguration as first US President in 1889. Six years later the wooden arch was replaced with the splendid marble one that remains today. The centerpiece of many political (and mock-political) demonstrations over the years, the arch achieved its greatest fame in 1917, when artist Marcel Duchamp and friends climbed to its crown to drunkenly declare the creation of New Bohemia.

Centered around Washington Square Park, **New York University** has had a profound influence on life in downtown Manhattan since its founding in 1831. The most obvious physical influence is the massive red block on the park's southeast corner, the Bobst Library, designed by Philip Johnson in the 1970s.

79

Little Italy

Once rich in sights, sounds, and fragrances typical of the Italian homeland, Little Italy has by now lost a lot of that cultural authenticity still possessed by nearby Chinatown. Recalling the neighborhood's roots, nevertheless, are still some small workshops and the restaurants and Italian grocers'—and of course, the flamboyant San Gennaro celebrations in mid-September. Don't forget to stop in at Umberto's Clam House, the restaurant where the Mafia killer Joey Gallo was gunned down in 1972 and where a bullet hole in the back door to the kitchen still recalls the event.

Some years ago, something like the old vitality began to flow back into Little Italy, especially in the area between Houston and Spring Streets, now known as **NoLiTa** (NOrth of Little ITAly), where you will find boutiques and restaurants catering mainly to a young, trendy clientele. The most interesting of the neighborhood's buildings is the Old Police Headquarters, built in classical Baroque style in 1909 at 240 Center Street, which later became famous as the Office of the Commissioner of Police of New York, Theodore Roosevelt. In 1988, the domed structure was transformed into a luxury condo that is presently the home of many representatives of the smart set. The red-brick Puck Building is, instead, a masterpiece of fin-de-siècle architecture on Lafayette Street and East Houston.

Chinatown

New York's Chinatown is the largest community of Chinese in the Western hemisphere, home to 150,000 immigrants from all over Asia. While San Francisco's Chinatown is more a focal point in that city's milieu, New York's Chinatown is still a favored destination of tourists and townies alike. The first immigrants to Chinatown were primarily Cantonese railroad workers from the West, who settled during the 1870s in a fairly proscribed, thirteen-block neighborhood centered around the terminus of Manhattan Bridge. Not much has changed since then, although the population surged in the 1970s after Congress increased Asian immigration quotas. The area remains rather insular, with some residents never speaking a word of English.

Chinatown is noisy and garish and jam-packed with people. The atmosphere is fast-paced and fun. The real draw here is cheap, delicious food: there are over 350 restaurants and numerous shops loaded with fresh fish and Chinese vegetables. Chinatown has twenty-seven banks and a host of municipal and criminal justice buildings, to give you an idea of the landscape. Given the neighborhood's present civic nature, it's hard to believe that in the nineteenth century this area was marked by the infamous Five Corners, one of the most murderous, gang-ridden slums in Manhattan. The bronze statue of Confucius in Confucius Plaza symbolizes the traditional Chinese values that dominate local politics.

*Two views of the **United Nations** headquarters on the East River.*

United Nations

Chartered in San Francisco in May of 1945, the United Nations opened its doors in New York City in 1952. In the spirit of Woodrow Wilson's League of Nations, which was stymied by post-World War I isolationist national politics, the United Nations was formed after World War II to protect world peace and humanitarian ideals. Today, the 189 member nations are allied to resolve international conflicts and safeguard human rights. The U.N.'s New York City address can be attributed almost entirely to the efforts of Nelson Rockefeller, the grandson of oil tycoon John D. Rockefeller and later Governor of New York State. As custodian of Rockefeller Center, Nelson Rockefeller wanted more than anything else to insure the prosperity of his holding. World politics aside, Nelson realized that by securing the U.N. midtown along the East River, he could both increase the value of Rockefeller Center, a mere ten blocks away from the proposed illustrious institution, and nullify the threat of a rival business center being constructed there. With an $8.5 million donation from his father, John D. Rockefeller, Jr., Nelson was able to buy the foul-smelling neighborhood of slaughterhouses along the river from developer William Zeckendorf. Subsequently, he was also able to convince the U.N. to set up shop in New York City. All in all, the U.N. is an 18-acre international zone complete with its own security force, fire department, translation center, post office, and printing plant, which happens to be one of the world's largest. The U.N. complex stretches from East 42nd Street to East 48th Street in a park that extends from First Avenue to the river.

The process of designing the U.N. was an example of international cooperation at its best. The American architect Wallace Harrison headed a ten-person board whose members included France's Le Corbusier, Brazil's Oscar Niemeyer, and Sweden's Sven Markelius.

Arts and artifacts donated by various countries suggest the scope of U.N. membership. Of special note, Henry Moore's sculpture *Reclining Figure: Hand* in the courtyard, and works by Chagall and Picasso, André Derain and Albert Marquet.

*The **New York Stock Exchange**, the world's most
important trading floor.*

*City Hall, built between 1802 and 1811 in the
neoclassical style so popular in that era.*

Wall Street

The homeland of American capitalism, Wall Street represents the core of New York's financial district. Wall Street got its name four centuries ago when Dutch settlers erected a wall on the northern side of the thoroughfare as protection from the local Indians. Founded in 1792 under a buttonwood tree, at the corner of Wall and Broad Streets, the **New York Stock Exchange** is now the trading ground for over 200 million shares a day.

The Exchange's raucous, capricious stock auction can be viewed from a gallery above during trading hours, 9:15 a.m. to 4:00 p.m., Monday through Friday. **Trinity Church** offers solace to those weary of Wall Street's more voracious aspects. The present Trinity Church was built on the site in 1846.

The first was constructed in 1698 under William and Mary's royal English charter. Trinity Church founded two of New York's most prestigious academic institutions, the Trinity School and Columbia University, formerly King's College. The church used to appear much more admonishing to those tempted by Wall Street's materialism, but recent restoration washed away the grime and brought back the sandstone's original rosy hue. The building is rather humble in size and ornamentation, although the steepled belltower, bronze doors, stained-glass windows, and exquisitely carved marble altar allude to its historical significance. The mossy cemetery in the back is home to the remains of such historical luminaries as Alexander Hamilton, Francis Lewis, and Robert Fulton.

Brooklyn Bridge

The world's first steel suspension bridge, the Brooklyn Bridge links Manhattan to Brooklyn and, at 5,989 feet (ca. 1826 m) long and 278 feet tall (nearly 85 m), is quite impressive even today. The bridge was designed in 1869 by Prussian immigrant John Roebling, who developed a form of wire rope for use on canal barges that was strong enough to employ on larger structures such as bridges. These cables, along with other engineering breakthroughs like iron trussing, gave the bridge a sense of weightless suspension that contrasts vividly with the mountainous Gothic stone towers through which the roadway runs.

The bridge took fourteen years and $15 million to build, not to mention that construction claimed twenty lives, most lost when the two 3,400-ton caissons were lowered into the riverbed to create a foundation. Another casualty was Roebling himself, who died of complications after his foot was crushed by a ferry while he was surveying the site. His son Washington took over the project, which he completed from sickbed with his wife Emily in charge.

The bridge was opened to the public on May 24, 1883 with much fanfare. A one-and-a-half mile (2.4 km) pedestrian ramp has unfortunately replaced the original walkway, but the bridge still offers an exhilarating stroll with amazing views of lower Manhattan.

*Some views of the **Brooklyn Bridge**.*

*Following pages: **Lower Manhattan** seen from the Brooklyn side of the East River, before September 11, 2001.*

Battery Park at the southern tip of Manhattan Island.

Battery Park

Battery Park is the mile-long (1.6 km) stretch of green built on landfill at the southern tip of Manhattan with sweeping views of the Financial District to the north, the Statue of Liberty and New York Harbor to the south, and the Hudson River to the east. The park is also the stomping ground for many street performers, who on the Admiral George Dewey Promenade play to the crowds waiting for ferries to Ellis Island.

The Park extends along the western shore from Chambers Street in TriBeCa all the way to the Battery, which is marked by the Castle Clinton National Monument. To illustrate how the Manhattan shoreline has changed, consider that the fort sat 300 feet (over 90 m) offshore when it was built in 1811 to deter the British navy in the War of 1812. It must have been quite a deterrent, because the Battery never fired a shot in wartime. Later on the Battery was converted into a concert hall and then an aquarium. Finally, in 1941, the fort became a historic monument with a small museum attached.

Dioramas inside show how the shoreline, and the fort itself, have changed. The well-manicured park is studded with many other statues and monuments. In 1909 a statue of Giovanni da Verrazzano was erected, allowing the explorer to gaze upon the bridge in the distance that bears his name. Hope Garden memorializes those who have died of AIDS, while a World War II monument features a huge sculpture of a soaring raptor set amid granite cenotaphs bearing the names of those who died on the Atlantic. A memorial flagpole, given to the city by the Dutch government, commemorates Peter Minuit's 1626 purchase of Manhattan Island from the Canarsee tribe.

The World Financial Center, in another stretch of Battery Park, includes the Winter Garden, a glass-roofed performing arts space, as well as an esplanade, yacht harbor, ice rink, and several plazas. The center, which integrates commercial and public spaces, was artfully master-minded by architects Alexander Cooper and Stanton Eckhut.

South Street Seaport

A re-creation of New York's historic nineteenth-century seaport, South Street Seaport's greatest lure is its beautiful riverfront setting. There are many enticing shops, bars, and restaurants, to be sure, but the location along Manhattan's southeastern shore is reason enough to investigate. The financial district's impressive skyline towers behind, and the Brooklyn Bridge looms out over the harbor, where a fleet of old-time tall ships is moored and open to the public. The Seaport Museum has several hands-on nautical exhibits, including a nineteenth-century print shop and a boat builder's shop. The Fulton Fish Market is the country's oldest fish market and it remains a messy, smelly throw-back to its glory days. Pier 17 has an expansive deck filled with lounge chairs from which to take in the marvelous river view.

*Three views of the **South Street Seaport**, New York's historical landing.*

Ellis Island and the Museum of Immigration

Ellis Island, over time the gateway to America for some sixteen million immigrants, is now home to a museum that traces their journeys from far-away homelands. Audiovisual, photographic, and text displays show how various groups of people, from Europeans to Asians to Africans, managed to end up in the New World.

Named after Samuel Ellis, the farmer who owned it, Ellis Island was once actually two islands that were joined and enlarged by landfill. Once a military outpost, the island became an immigrant-receiving station in 1892, when it became clear that Castle Clinton in Battery Park was ill-equipped to accommodate the throngs of foreign arrivals. At its busiest, Ellis Island welcomed 5,000 immigrants a day. Since first-class passengers were permitted to disembark directly in Manhattan, the majority of those interned at Ellis were poor. Each was interviewed and given a medical checkup to ferret out those who might become "public charges," although only about two percent were turned away. Frank Capra, Bela Lugosi, and Rudolph Valentino were but a few who entered America across this threshold. The present museum was refurbished in 1986 through the efforts of a centennial committee headed by Chrysler automobile chairman Lee Iacocca, son of immigrants who arrived at Ellis.

Statue of Liberty

The 250-ton, 151-foot (46-meter) statue was born of the efforts of three Frenchmen: the historian Edouard-René de Labolaye conceived of the idea, Frédéric-Auguste Bartholdi sculpted the statue, and Alexandre-Gustave Eiffel, creator of the eponymous tower in Paris, engineered its supporting structure. Bartholdi's Lady Liberty took ten years to sculpt and the copper plates were completed in 1874. The statue was erected through the efforts of *New York World* editor Joseph Pulitzer, who garnered support and funding on the American front to complete the pedestal, and was dedicated on October 28, 1886. In her left hand, Lady Liberty holds the Declaration of Independence; in her right she bears the famous torch. The chains of tyranny are seen trampled beneath her feet as a symbol of freedom for the people of all seven continents, represented by the seven points of her crown. Emma Lazarus' poem, *The New Colossus,* is engraved on the statue's base and entrenched in the annals of American history. Lady Liberty is colossal in every aspect. Climb the 171 steps to the top and you've had a workout equivalent to a twenty-two story ascent. Pedestal included, the tip top soars 305 feet (93 m) above New York Harbor. In 1986 the statue underwent extensive centennial restoration that left it standing more proudly than ever. Several sections of the copper were replaced, and, most notably, the torch regained to the original gold-leaf splendor of Bartholdi's design. The viewing decks on the statue's feet and crown are open to visitors, but prepare for long waits for both.